Kiplinger's

Build A Winning Portfolio

Investment Strategies for Meeting Your Financial Goals

Peter J. Tanous

KAPLAN PUBLISHING

New York

This publication is designed to provide accurate and authoritative information in regard to the subject matter covered. It is sold with the understanding that the publisher is not engaged in rendering legal, accounting, or other professional service. If legal advice or other expert assistance is required, the services of a competent professional should be sought.

Vice President and Publisher: Maureen McMahon
Editorial Director: Jennifer Farthing
Acquisitions Editor: Shannon Berning
Development Editor: Monica P. Lugo
Production Editor: Dominique Polfliet
Production Designer: Todd Bowman
Cover Designer: Carly Schnur

© 2008 Peter J. Tanous

Published by Kaplan Publishing, a division of Kaplan, Inc.
1 Liberty Plaza, 24th Floor
New York, NY 10006

All rights reserved. The text of this publication, or any part thereof, may not be reproduced in any manner whatsoever without written permission from the publisher.

Printed in the United States of America

January 2008
10 9 8 7 6 5 4 3 2 1

ISBN-13: 978-1-4277-9621-9

Kaplan Publishing books are available at special quantity discounts to use for sales promotions, employee premiums, or educational purposes. Please email our Special Sales Department to order or for more information at *kaplanpublishing@kaplan.com,* or write to Kaplan Publishing, 1 Liberty Plaza, 24th Floor, New York, NY 10006.

Contents

For
Olivia Rose Bartilucci
Isabella Grace Bartilucci
Lilly Catherine Bartilucci

Beauty Seen Is Never Lost
John Greenleaf Whittier
(1807–1892)

What You Should Expect to Get Out of This Book

We are about to embark together on a financial journey.

You've picked up this book because you are interested in building a portfolio of securities. You might want a portfolio that will grow for 20 years or longer, one that will ensure a comfortable or even luxurious retirement. Or maybe you want to save up for an expensive education for your children. You might be looking to start a new business and you need to accumulate some capital over 5 or 10 years to get there. Perhaps you are looking to buy a fancy yacht or a condo at the beach.

These are all excellent goals—destinations, if you will. My job is to guide you through the investment journey so you can reach your goals. So, what are my qualifications? Aside from being the author of three other investment books, I have over 40 years of financial experience. I run an investment consulting company that advises on over $1 billion in assets for individuals, families, and institutions like endowments, pension plans, colleges, and schools. My firm is in a branch of the investment business that few individuals ever come across: investment consulting. Firms like ours are hired by wealthy individuals and institutions to help them build portfolios and select the managers to invest each part of the portfolio. We then monitor the performance of the managers and hire and fire accordingly. We get paid a fee for our services since we don't accept compensation from any of the managers or funds we recommend. Consulting firms use a variety of sophisticated tools designed to assist in the portfolio building process. I will share some of these tools with you in a way that will allow you to build your own portfolio with the help of state-of-the-art techniques in managing money. I will on occasion introduce you to some of the principles of modern portfolio theory. MPT, as we refer to it, was pioneered by Harry Markowitz who won the Nobel Memorial Prize in Economics for his work in studying the effects of risk and diversification on portfolios. Much of what we use in building portfolios today was based on Markowitz's work, as well as the work of others who followed him.

I hasten to add that I am not going to embark on long academic dissertations that would put all of us to sleep. I will instead pick out some gems of knowledge that I want to share with you and I think you will enjoy. These principles will help explain why we look at investments in certain ways and this knowledge will help cement in your mind the principles of solid and intelligent investing. None of what I will cover requires any special education or training on your part. The portfolio I will help you build is one that will be tailor-made for you and we'll build it piece by piece. You will learn the importance of diversification, risk, and balance, and we'll stress what really counts in investments—and what doesn't. You may well be surprised!

As we go along, I will cover the topics that are essential to creating a winning portfolio. I'll address what a portfolio is, risk in investments, and asset allocation.

Later on, we will address the important topic of whether you should pick stocks or buy a mutual fund and let the fund manager pick the stocks for you. This may be the most frequently debated topic in the investment community. Are you better off buying a mutual fund that might beat the market or should you buy an index fund and have the satisfaction that you will get the market's return, whatever it happens to be? Or should you buy both? I wrote an entire book on this subject through interviews with noted investment gurus and leading academics in the field, including two Nobel Prize winners in economics. We'll have a go at it too. I will also address the question of whether or not you should use a financial advisor, the process of assembling the components of a portfolio, and keeping your assets safe, as well as some powerful modeling techniques used by investment professionals to predict a range of returns for a specific portfolio.

I intend to make our journey interesting, educational and even fun, because that's the way I like to learn new things. But before we proceed, a promise: I will not insult your intelligence by claiming to reveal stock market "secrets" or hidden strategies that are guaranteed to make you rich. Yes, there have been plenty of books with claims like that, but as I suspect you know, these secret formulas and strategies are right up there in credibility with books on alchemy and fortune telling. There are sensible ways to build a fortune in the market, and over the years professionals in our field have accumulated a wealth of information on what works in the investment business, and what doesn't. There is some new thinking on the subject of portfolio construction as well, and I will cover it with you.

Are you ready? When you are, turn the page and let's get started!

What's a Portfolio?

Chapter 1

If our mission is to build a winning portfolio, we ought to start by agreeing on what a portfolio is. A portfolio is composed of a variety of different investments with different characteristics designed to enhance the overall investment returns and reduce the risk in the process. The reason we want to build a portfolio is that experience has taught us that different types of investments have different peculiarities and performance histories.

For our purposes, we will define a portfolio as a collection of different investments, mostly in stocks and bonds and other liquid (readily marketable) investment vehicles. Let's start with some basic details on each of these.

What's a Stock?

Stock, also called *shares* or *equity,* represents ownership in a company. Here's a simple illustration: Suppose you start a company and incorporate it where you live, say, in Iowa. Your company makes ladders. You make terrific ladders, in fact, and are very successful with your highly portable and ultra-light aluminum model. You decide you need some capital to expand

The reason we want to build a portfolio is that experience has taught us that different types of investments have different peculiarities and performance histories.

the business and build a small ladder-making factory. You figure you'll need about $100,000 and the bank will lend you the rest. But you don't have $100,000. So you decide to find friends and relatives who want to invest in your company. Let's see, you ask, how much of the company should I give them for $100,000? How about one-half. Well, if you are going to sell half the company for $100,000, that makes the entire company worth $200,000, at least to you.

So you ask your lawyer to divide the company into shares of stock. The entire company will consist of 200 shares of stock. If the company is worth $200,000, then each share will be worth $1,000. So what you have done is break up the company into 200 pieces of ownership, and each piece is represented by a stock certificate, which represents ownership of one share of the company, each share representing 1 percent ownership of the company.

Word to the wise: Don't go around selling stock to your friends and neighbors, or you are likely to get into a bit of trouble with the Securities and Exchange Commission (SEC), which regulates stock trading. If your company grows to a point where it is appropriate to raise money from the public at large, you are likely to get a call from a securities underwriter, maybe Smith Barney, Goldman Sachs, or Merrill Lynch, if they deem that your company is worth their attention. They will assess the demand for your company's stock, file the lengthy registration statement with the SEC, take you on the road to tell investors about how wonderful your company is, and finally launch it in the market through an initial public offering (IPO). After that, you will be somewhat famous, at least in the business community, and if your company's stock qualifies, its stock is likely to be listed on the New York Stock Exchange, or the NASDAQ market.

Why Do Stocks Go Up or Down?

There have been many books written about why stocks go up or down. The most simple, and somewhat smart-aleck answer, is that stocks go up because there are more buyers than sellers: supply and demand, Economics 101. If more people want to buy something, stocks or anything else, the demand will bid the price up. Conversely, if some goods are for sale and there are more people who want to sell than there are buyers, the sellers will force the price down. Name any item, it's the same story—cars, houses, stocks. But this explanation doesn't get at the heart of the matter.

The single most important reason that stocks go up is that corporate earnings are going up. Yes, it is that simple. Even during the crazy days of the Internet bubble in the late 1990s, when Internet stocks with no earnings at all were selling at astronomical prices, the reason those stocks went up was that investors *thought* there would be high earnings from these companies in the future. In most cases they were wrong and the stocks came crashing to earth, but great (and unrealistic) hope for earnings was what propelled those stock prices into the stratosphere. So even without the ability to see into the future, it is safe to assume that as long as the American economy continues to grow, and corporate earnings continue to increase, stock prices will continue to rise.

Types of Stocks

When we talk about stocks, we are, consciously or not, almost always referring to common stocks. Common stocks are the ones that represent ownership in the underlying company. But common stocks aren't the only kind of stocks. There is another type of stock called *preferred stock.*

The single most important reason that stocks go up is that corporate earnings are going up. Yes, it is that simple.

3

Preferred stocks are much more like bonds than they are like common stocks. Companies can issue a number of different securities, and there is a hierarchy of securities, ranging from the most senior to the most junior. At the top of the hierarchy, the Lion King of securities if you will, are bonds, which are an IOU to the investor from the company. Next in the hierarchy are preferred stocks. When they are issued, they have a fixed dividend; say 5 percent or 6 percent. The company pays the dividend at regular intervals and, because of this, these stocks are more like bonds. They do not fluctuate based on the company's earnings. Their prices tend to move with changes in interest rates. It is not likely you will own any of these in your portfolio, but it is useful to know what they are all the same.

Styles of Stocks

Another very important characteristic of different types of stocks is style, only this is isn't the fashion variety of style. The two basic styles among stocks are Value and Growth.

Value Stocks Value stock investors are bargain hunters. You shop at Bloomingdales; they shop at Filene's Basement. These are people looking for dollar bills they can buy for 65 cents. Think about the high school dances you attended. There were those people who were not necessarily glamorous or outgoing, whose qualities were more hidden and harder to discover—the wallflowers. These are the value stocks, hidden treasures whose virtues and qualities don't scream at you but are nevertheless there, waiting to be found.

So they're generally cheap, they sometimes sell at prices below the real value of their assets, and they have fallen on hard times—the stock is probably as low as it is going to get. The question is What is going to make the stock go up? An interesting question indeed. Value investors often look for an additional element when they consider buying a value stock: a catalyst. A catalyst is that something special that will turn the fortunes of this particular company around. Without it, you might buy an undervalued company that stays undervalued for a very long time. You can't make much money that way. A catalyst might be a takeover by another company or by one of those private equity funds seeking a bargain or it might be new management that is determined to turn the company's fortunes around, or even a new plan to maximize the value of the company's hidden assets. Whatever it is, value investors like the comfort of identifying something that is likely to happen that will make the stock go up.

Growth Stocks Growth stocks are very different from value stocks. These are not the wallflowers at the dance, but the stars. Think of John Travolta in *Saturday Night Fever,* the white suit, the dance floor, the Bee Gees—you get the picture. Growth stocks get attention because they are companies that consistently grow in sales and earnings. Isn't that what every investor wants? Think about the growth stocks you have known over time, even if you didn't actually own the stocks—Coca-Cola, Microsoft, Intel, General Electric, and so on. What these companies have in common is that they grow year by year with almost no interruptions. And if the sales and earnings keep growing, isn't it reasonable to expect that the stock price will continue to grow too? Yes it is. And over time, that's pretty much what happens.

Determining How Much Stocks Are "Worth"

If a growth stock sells for $50 a share and a value stock sells for $10 dollars a share, does that mean that the growth stock is selling at a higher price? In investment terms, not necessarily.

Price Earnings Ratio To even the playing field, we have to come up with a way to compare the price levels of all these different stocks. The most important way we do that is through the price earnings ratio. This is often referred to as the P/E, or even as the *multiple*. Let's have a closer look.

If I have to compare two stocks and how "cheap" or "expensive" they are, the best way for me to do that is *not* to compare what the stock price is selling for, but what the price earnings ratio is. For example, if one company's stock is selling at 50 and another at 10, it may be that the company whose stock is selling for 10 has more shares outstanding or higher earnings than the one selling at 50. But if that's the case, how do I compare them? Here's how: To put this on an even playing field, you divide the price of the stock by the company's earnings per share. (The earnings per share is the net earnings of the company divided by the total amount of shares outstanding.) So if company A is selling for $50 a share and has per share earnings of $5, we say that it is selling at a price earnings ratio of 10 times earnings, which is the share price of $50 divided by the per share earnings of $5. Ten times earnings is considered a pretty reasonable price earnings ratio.

If company B's stock is selling at $10 per share and it has earnings per share of $0.50, then it is selling at a price earnings ratio of 20 times earnings, which is 10 divided by 0.50. A price earnings ratio of 20 times earnings makes this stock more "expensive" than the company whose stock sells at 10 times earnings. So the most expensive stock isn't the one that sells for $50 a share; that stock just sells at a higher price. From a valuation point of view, the stock that is selling at $10 a share is actually the more expensive one since it sells at a higher price earnings ratio, that is, 20 times earnings versus 10 times earnings, than the stock that sells at $50 a share.

The theory here is that a higher price earnings ratio means that we are willing to pay more for the earnings of this company than we are for another one. The average price earnings ratio for the Standard & Poor's 500 stock index is around 16 times earnings. If a stock has a high price earnings ratio, it is because investors have a lot of confidence that the company is going to continue to grow at a rapid pace. One formula for evaluating price earnings ratios is that the P/E should be equivalent to the growth rate. In other words, if a company is growing at 10 percent a year, it ought to have a P/E of 10 times earnings. A growth rate of 20 percent merits a P/E of 20 times earnings, and so on.

It stands to reason then that a company that is growing slowly is going to have a lower P/E than a company that is growing rapidly. The stock market historically pays more for growth.

How Big Is Your Company? There are companies of all sizes whose stocks you can buy, from the tiny little start-up companies to the huge mega companies that are household names, like General Electric, General Motors, Coca-Cola, IBM, and so on. These big companies are called *large capitalization stocks,* or *large cap* for short. (Capitalization refers to the total market value of the company as measured by the number of shares outstanding times the stock price.) Small company stocks are called *small cap* and there is also the in-between category of companies known as *mid cap*.

How much are these different categories of companies worth? There are no hard and fast rules, but generally speaking, large-cap companies have capitalizations of $8 billion or more, mid-cap companies $3 to $8 billion, and small-cap companies are those whose market values are under $3 billion.

The reason it is important to focus on the size of the companies whose stocks you may be considering is that, like the growth and value stocks, large-cap and small-cap stocks tend to have different performance characteristics as a group. Interestingly, in the early part of this century, small-cap stocks have trounced large-cap stocks in performance. From 2000 to 2006, which includes the three-year decline in 2000, 2001, and 2002, large-cap stocks gained an average of 1.67 percent a year, while small-cap stocks rose 7.91 percent. The chart on the following page shows how each category of stocks, large and small, performed during those years.

This chart clearly shows that during this period, small-cap stocks outperformed their large-cap brethren. The problem is that we can't really predict when these periods of outperformance and underperformance will occur.

Why Are Stocks So Important for a Portfolio?
Throughout the history of the United States, common stocks have been the best-performing asset class of all, better than gold, better than real estate, better than commodities, and a whole lot better than bonds. Take a look at the second chart on page 10. It shows the growth of stocks, bonds and inflation in the United States since 1925.

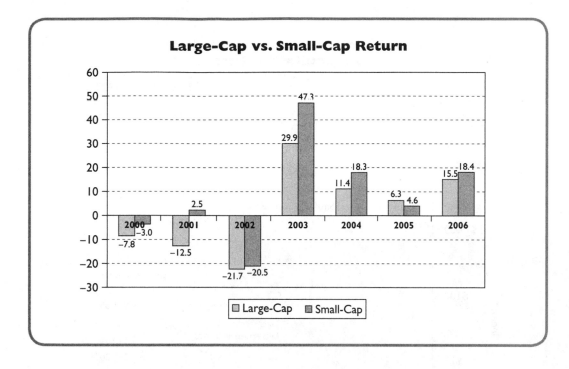

Let's assume your wise old grandparents invested $1,000 in Treasury bills for you back in 1925. At the end of 2006, you would have had over $70,000, thanks to their generosity. But suppose instead that your grandparents invested in some big company stocks, the equivalent of the S&P 500 index. Had they done that, you would today be worth over $3 million, yes that much, from a $1,000 investment. True, $1,000 back then was roughly equivalent to $10,000 today, but the results are still mighty impressive.

Think about all of the events that have transpired since 1925. The biggest was, of course, the stock market crash of 1929 and the Great Depression. During that time, your portfolio would have suffered some immense trauma, but if you had remained steadfast, better days would eventually come. Over the years, your portfolio also survived World War II, the Korean War, the Kennedy

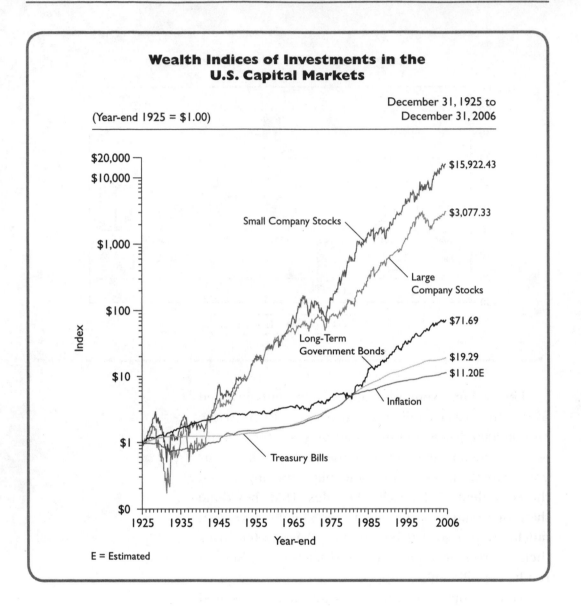

Wealth Indices of Investments in the U.S. Capital Markets

(Year-end 1925 = $1.00)

December 31, 1925 to
December 31, 2006

$20,000
$10,000 — $15,922.43

$3,077.33

Small Company Stocks

$1,000

Large
Company Stocks

$100

$71.69

Long-Term
Government Bonds

$19.29
$11.20E

$10

Inflation

$1

Treasury Bills

$0

1925 1935 1945 1955 1965 1975 1985 1995 2006

Year-end

Index

E = Estimated

assassination, and 9/11, and through all of those calamities, your portfolio kept growing. It did not grow in a nice straight line, of course; there were ups and downs. But grow it did, enough to make you very rich. All this because grandpa and grandma invested $1,000 for you in 1925. The conclusion you draw from this history is that if you want your money to grow, stocks are likely the way to go. History is on our side, the track record is long, and there is simply nothing else that comes close.

Why Are the Style and Size of Stocks So Important? Over time, stocks of different styles perform differently from one another. Say you only own growth stocks. Most investors, if asked, would rather own a stock in companies that are growing than in those whose progress is slow, or even sluggish. That's pretty logical. So what's the catch? The catch is that you pay a price for that high growth in the form of the high price-earnings ratio. And is that bad? The problem with a high P/E is that it *assumes* that the growth is going to continue. And if for some reason the growth is interrupted, the high price-earnings ratio is no longer justified and the stock comes tumbling down. Happens all the time. That's why most savvy investors want to own both growth and value stocks.

Stocks of different styles and sizes perform differently from one another, and a well-diversified portfolio will inevitably have both growth and value stocks, and large- and small-cap stocks, in it. We'll get more into the reasons why this is important from a risk management point of view in the next chapter.

> **For those who want others to do the stock picking for them, there are mutual funds.**

What's a Mutual Fund?

Some people buy stocks they've researched and like. Others don't want to be bothered. For those who want others to do the stock picking for them, there are mutual funds. Mutual funds are pooled investment vehicles. For example, a mutual fund may own hundreds of different stocks of different companies. An investor can buy a share of a mutual fund and own his proportional share of all the stocks in the fund. Buying shares in a mutual fund is a terrific way to own hundreds of stocks that you might not otherwise be able to afford to buy. It also offers diversification, a key element to a winning portfolio.

Types of Mutual Funds

There are two types of mutual funds: closed end and open end.

Open End When you buy shares, the mutual fund just issues new shares to you, takes your money, and invests it in the fund. Most of the funds you will have heard of, such as the Fidelity or Vanguard family of funds, are open ended. They are priced every day based on the closing value of the shares of stock the fund owns. You can buy or sell shares of the fund based on the fund's closing price each day the stock market is open. Open-end funds are far more numerous and popular than closed-end funds.

Closed End Closed-end funds have a fixed number of shares and trade like stocks. A closed-end fund is offered to investors much the same way a stock is offered, with a fixed number of shares at a specific offering price. If the offering price is, say, $10 a share, that money (less the fees) along with the investments of the other shareholders, will buy the stocks in the company that the manager selects. The difference between closed end and open end is that after the initial offering of an open-ended fund, if a new investor comes along and wants to buy, or even if an existing investor wants to add to her holdings, the open-ended fund will just issue new shares and take her money.

A closed-end fund has no more shares to issue. Its shares may well be listed on an exchange, like the New

MUTUAL FUND FEES

Somewhere there is an individual of enormous complexity who enjoys creating puzzles that defy normal analysis or logic. That person, or one of his relatives, also made a business of devising fees charged to investors who buy mutual funds. If exposed fully, this topic might fill its own book, but who would read it?

Load and No-Load

Here are the basics: There are two types of funds—load and no-load. Load funds charge fees up front, as high as 5 percent. So if you invest in one, 5 cents out of every dollar goes for fees and you are starting with only 95 cents invested. Load-fund fees pay commission to the selling broker. The brokers like load funds. Guess why? No-load funds do not charge an upfront fee, or sales commission. All of the money you invest gets invested in the fund.

Expense Ratio

This is a fancy term for what the expenses of the fund are as a percentage of the total assets of the fund. An equity (stock) fund might have an expense ratio of 1.5 percent.

That money is charged annually by the fund to cover the costs of its operations. An index fund, which mirrors the performance of the stock market by tracking a well-known index, like the S&P 500, has a very low expense ratio, usually under 0.25 percent.

Share Class

Mutual funds sometimes have three classes of shares, A, B, and C. These different classes of shares determine how the commission they charge are paid. In some cases, as in load funds, it all comes out at the time you invest. In other cases, the fees are deducted annually for a period of time. There is a great deal of creativity involved in the fee structure designed to ensure that the promoters and managers of mutual funds earn a good living from your investment. If they earn it by delivering good performance, no one is unhappy. We will explore how to evaluate and pick mutual funds while keeping an eye on fees. The bottom line is that some of these fees are unnecessary and, in general, there is little reason to buy a load fund.

York Stock Exchange, and the price of the shares will generally reflect the value of the securities in the portfolio. So if the market value of the holdings in the fund average out to $10 a share, the stock should sell in the market for about that amount.

The problem is that it often doesn't sell for its true, or book, value. Closed-end funds often sell at a discount to their real value. In this case, the stock might sell at $9 a share (even though the value of the underlying stocks is closer to $10 a share) because of supply and demand. There just aren't enough buyers who want to pay $10 a share. So the seller has to take whatever he can get and that usually means a lower price. Most investors will not own closed-end funds, but here again, this is something you should know about.

What's a Bond?

Let's go back to our ladder company example. You decide you don't really want to sell ownership in your ladder company. You started it and you want to own the whole darn thing yourself. But you still need capital. You decide that instead of selling stock, or equity, in your company, you will instead borrow money from those friends and relatives. To borrow the money, you issue bonds. These are certificates that don't offer ownership, they are just an IOU. Since you are borrowing money, you will have to pay interest on the money you borrow at, say, 6 percent a year. So the bond is said to have a coupon of 6 percent. If you follow the pattern of most bonds, twice a year you will deliver a check to the bondholders of 6 percent annualized (so twice a year you would give them 3 percent) in interest. The bonds will have a maturity that you will have agreed on with the investors, perhaps 10 years. That means that in addition to the interest you are paying them every six months, you will give them their original investment back in 10 years.

What's the Difference between Stocks and Bonds?

The main difference between stocks and bonds is that with stock you own a piece of the company. So if the company increases in value, the value of your stock will go up. Likewise, if the company falls on hard times, the value of your stock will go down. That's why stocks fluctuate.

With a bond, you don't own a piece of the company; the company simply owes you money that they have to pay you in good times or bad. And if they don't? If the company misses a single interest payment, you can put them out of business. So bonds are considered far more secure than stocks, and if the company goes bankrupt, the bondholders will have first claim on any remaining assets and the stockholders will likely end up with nothing. That's why bonds are often refereed to as *senior securities*.

Types of Bonds

I mentioned earlier that a bond is the Lion King of investments. But there is also a hierarchy among these lions of the investment jungle.

Secured Bonds At the top of the heap you will find secured bonds. These bonds have a claim on all of the assets of the company. Here's a quick example: If your company goes bankrupt, the bondholders have a first claim on the assets. However, the *secured* bondholders get first dibs on the assets. Say the company has a factory that will be sold at the bankruptcy auction. The proceeds of that sale go exclusively to the secured bondholders until they are paid in full.

Unsecured Bonds Next in line are unsecured bonds. These bondholders will get paid before any of the

> With a bond, you don't own a piece of the company; the company simply owes you money that they have to pay you in good times or bad.

stockholders get anything but have no claim on any particular assets. After they have been paid, assuming there is anything left over, the preferred stockholders (if there are any) get paid back, and finally, last in line are the common stockholders. They usually wind up with nothing. That's what happens when you're last in line.

Convertible Bonds Want the best of all investment worlds? Have a look at convertible bonds. You'll soon refer to them as *converts*. These bonds are unsecured bonds, so they are low on the bond totem pole, but they are still bonds and therefore ahead of all of the classes of stock in the corporate hierarchy. And they have a great additional feature: They can be converted into stock at a specified price. What that means is that your bond might have a yield of 5 percent based on its interest rate, but you can convert it into shares for a specific period of time. For example, let's say that your Acme bond is convertible into 10 shares of Acme stock. Most bonds are issued at $1,000. Acme stock is selling around $100 per share. Since your bond is convertible into 10 shares of Acme stock at $100 per share, $1,000 is the right price.

But what if Acme stock goes up? The company is earning more money than anyone expected, and investors bid the stock up to $120 a share. How much is your bond worth now? Well, since you can convert that bond into 10 shares of Acme stock, it will be worth 120 times 10, or $1,200. Best of both worlds. You get the income from the bond and the capital appreciation if the stock price rises.

So why doesn't every investor want to buy a lot of convertibles? For one thing, there are not very many of them. They are a good deal for the investor to be sure, but not so good for the company since the company has to pay interest and also issue shares if the stock price goes up. Therefore, companies that issue convertibles generally do so because they don't have a cheaper way to raise capital. That in turn suggests that these are not necessarily the best companies to invest in, but there are attractive investments to be found in this type of security.

Callable Bonds Many bonds, including convertible bonds, have what is known as a *call feature*. That means that even though the bond may be a 10-year bond, the company can "call it in," that is, redeem it by giving you your money back or a little more, earlier. The earliest date the company can exercise the call is the call date. For convertible bonds, the company can force you to convert if it wants to stop paying the interest on the bond. For example, if the bond is callable at 102 (that means $1,020 per bond), and the bond is selling at 120 ($1,200) because the Acme stock price went up, then you would exercise your right to convert the bond into stock worth $1,200 rather than sell it back to the company at $1,020 if the bond is called.

With regular bonds, companies will exercise the call feature if interest rates go down. For example, suppose Acme issued regular (not convertible) bonds with a 7 percent coupon (interest rate) and in the ensuing years interest rates went down to 5 percent. Well, they sure would look dumb paying 7 percent in that lower interest rate environment. So they call the bond in, pay you back your principal, and later issue new bonds at the lower prevailing interest rate of 5 percent.

Other Investments

There are other investments that might be included in your winning portfolio, depending on who you are and what your investment objectives happen to be. Here are some important "other" investments that we will be talking about.

Cash

When we talk about the "cash" component of a portfolio, it isn't the kind of cash we normally think about. That cash comes in different denominations of bills that we spend on groceries and in taxicabs. Some people also use it as savings by stuffing it in the proverbial mattress.

For your winning portfolio purposes, cash just means that amount of your portfolio that will be instantly (or almost instantly) liquid and available and won't be subject to any market fluctuations. In other words, no risk.

But that doesn't mean we aren't going to try to earn *something* on this liquid investment. You might think of cash as the money in your bank account. It might typically earn a little interest. In investment accounts, most large investment firms, like Smith Barney, Merrill Lynch, Fidelity, or Schwab, offer to pay you interest on the cash left in your account. The most sensible ways to handle this asset class is to invest it in a money market fund that might be offered by the brokerage firm you are dealing with. If taxes are an issue, the large firms also have tax-exempt money market funds that will hold your cash in tax-exempt securities. There is theoretically a little risk involved here but it is so minor that it should not be a concern at all.

Exchange Traded Funds (ETF)

Exchange traded funds, usually referred to as ETFs, are a relatively new form of mutual fund. ETFs are funds that are traded like stocks, which means that, unlike most mutual funds that you buy or sell once a day at the closing daily value, ETFs trade on a stock exchange and can be bought and sold any time during the trading day.

ETFs have many advantages. First of all, there are a great many of them, over 350 at this writing—more by the time you read this. They cover a range of possible investments that allow investors to invest in sectors and subsectors of an almost infinite number of industries and sectors. Want to invest in raw materials, health care, consumer staples, real estate, or a particular country? There's an ETF for you. They are also cost efficient. Most ETFs have relatively low expense ratios. If you are interested in tracking the stock market, an ETF that tracks the S&P 500 index charges only 0.12 percent.

Hedge Funds

The very name *hedge fund* sometimes provokes a shiver or some other visceral response on the part of many investors. Hedge funds are investment partnerships that engage in investment strategies that most mutual funds are unable to do. These include "going short," a practice of selling stock you don't own in order to make money when the stock goes down. The idea is that you'll buy the stock back at a lower price and earn the difference between what you sold it for at the higher price and what you pay to buy it back. It also includes the use of options and leverage, potentially risky strategies that can both increase your gain substantially, or increase your loss substantially depending on the talent of the manager running the fund.

Hedge funds are usually considered risky investments. Not all of them are risky, and we'll get into this in more detail in the chapter on asset allocation. Keep in mind that with hedge funds, investors are required to lock up their money for a period of time, sometimes as long as one or two years before they can get out.

Commodities

Some portfolios contain commodities in varying degrees. Commodities constitute a very specialized area of investment in such fields as corn, wheat, barley, and, yes, pork bellies. I will have some recommendations for your winning portfolio in commodities, although not in any of the aforementioned categories. Be assured, there are no pork bellies in your investing future!

The Case for Diversification

And why do we need all these different investments in the first place? Wouldn't it make sense to just buy a collection of good stocks, or a good mutual fund and be done with it? After all, grandma and grandpa didn't read a book when they made that $1,000 investment for you and that turned out just fine. So why shouldn't we just go ahead and do the same thing and be done with it?

There are a number of reasons. One is that I will assume you are not going to invest for the next 80 years and that your own time frame for investing is a lot shorter. In that case, we must be concerned about something the old folks weren't concerned about back in the 1920s: What happens in the meantime? If your investment time horizon is 10 years, another look at that chart will show that there are plenty of 10-year periods when investing in stocks wasn't a good idea and returns were meager or even negative. That is not an acceptable alternative for your retirement nest egg or your other investment goals. As a result, we have to find ways to mitigate the risk that ups and downs in the stock market won't ruin your investment plans.

That is what building a winning portfolio is really about. In a single word, it is about diversification. The first step in building a winning portfolio is assembling the pieces of the portfolio and understanding why diversification is important. If diversification didn't matter, we might just buy one mutual fund and a few stocks and be done with it. Bad idea. Likewise buying four or five mutual funds or stocks does not a good portfolio make if all of the funds and stocks are of the same style or size. Five growth stocks or growth mutual funds is not a diversified portfolio. There are reasons for building a portfolio intelligently using many of the principles of modern portfolio theory. Diversification is one of the most important principles and is the cornerstone of risk management.

Notice that I haven't even talked about stock or mutual fund selection yet. I haven't discussed how to find those great funds or managers who have the magic touch in picking investments. Why haven't I talked about that yet? Because it isn't as important as understanding diversification in building your winning portfolio.

In the next chapters I'll talk about what really matters in investments. The problem most of us face is that we are assaulted daily with too much financial information. It is very easy to be confused about what is important and what isn't. From an investment point of view, most of what we hear about investing is "noise," useless information which will not help in our investment plans one bit. Sadly, much of the information we think is important is not useful at all. In this category I include virtually all of the market predictions and analyses by the various "talking heads" on TV and radio and in the written media. Market newsletters are also pretty useless. What makes us think that any one of these has an inside track on predicting the future? Every so often someone will make a lucky call and live off it for years, but I know of no analyst with a consistent record of predicting the direction of the stock market. Yes, Warren Buffett

The first step in building a winning portfolio is assembling the pieces of the portfolio and understanding why diversification is important.

is a genius and he has made a huge amount of money investing, but when you get right down to it, most of what he does is common sense and he eagerly shares his thought process with the investors in his company, Berkshire Hathaway, and with the world. And there is only one Warren Buffett.

In one of my earlier books, *Investment Gurus,* I interviewed the most legendary mutual fund manager in history, Peter Lynch. Lynch had a track record running the Fidelity Magellan Fund that will likely never be beaten—29 percent a year for 13 years from 1977 to 1990. He has also written three very good investment books that tell you exactly how he did it! Yet when I lecture on investment, I sometimes ask the audience how many people have read any of Peter Lynch's books. Most of the time, a lot of hands go up. Then I ask how many people got rich following Peter Lynch's methods, which he explains carefully and very well in his books. The usual answer: no one. The simple explanation is not that Lynch writes bad books or that he left something out. The explanation is that there is only one Peter Lynch, and trying to imitate him is not going to work for most people. Instead, in this book I will teach you how to build a successful portfolio that is based on a solid foundation of academic and practical wisdom gained over the ages.

Let's Talk about Risk

f it weren't for risk, think about how our lives would be different! (I'll concentrate on the financial implications; you can fantasize about other areas if you care to.) If risk wasn't a consideration, this is the portfolio I would likely recommend for you:

Small-cap stocks	20%
Penny stocks	20%
Emerging-market stocks	20%
Volatile commodities	20%
New stock offerings (IPOs)	20%

And what fun we would have.

Now this portfolio might make a huge amount of money. For example, emerging markets have had stellar stock market performance over the past few years. The MSCI Emerging Markets index has appreciated by an annualized 27 percent for the five years ended in 2006. So who wouldn't want to own a lot of stocks in that category? Why shouldn't we own a portfolio that looks like this?

I think you know the answer: Because this portfolio is very risky. That means that it might do very well, as

When we consider risk in our investments, we are simply acknowledging the fact that we can't predict the future.

emerging markets and those other categories have done in the past, or they might suffer catastrophic losses. Think, for example, of the Internet boom and subsequent bubble in the late 1990s. The NASDAQ index, where most of those Internet stocks were traded, reached a peak on March 10, 2000, of 5048. Within a few months, the NASDAQ index sank over 37 percent to 3164 on May 23, 2000. And it was far from over. After that came dizzying decline to a low of 1114 on October 9, 2002, a decline of over 75 percent from the peak in 2000. Many investors, watching the stocks tumble, listened to some of the experts on Wall Street who pontificated that these declines were a terrific "buying opportunity." Then they watched the stocks tumble much, much further. It is likely that you, or someone you know, was caught up in this maelstrom. It is hard to buck the trend when everyone is having such a good time.

This is just one example of risk. When we consider risk in our investments, we are simply acknowledging the fact that we can't predict the future. At least most of us can't. I realize that there is a cottage industry of seers selling newsletters and other advice, and forecasters who appear on Bloomberg and CNBC, who are fond of telling us exactly what the market is likely to do. Sadly, there is no record of anyone being right about the future of the stock market *consistently*. Yes, there have been plenty of lucky calls, and those prognosticators managed to live off their calls for a long time. Unfortunately, the brilliant calls were rarely if ever repeated.

One celebrated example is analyst Elaine Garzarelli, who predicted the 1987 stock market crash, which was the worst single day stock market catastrophe since the crash of 1929. Black Monday, as it is called, happened on Monday, October 19, 1987, when the Dow Jones Industrial Average (DJIA) tumbled over 22 percent in a single day, causing similar major declines in markets around the world.

But it was surely good news for Ms. Garzarelli who became famous overnight for her prescient call. Of course, she has not made any similarly accurate forecasts since then. She did parlay her fame into a mutual fund she ran for seven years. During this time, her fund underperformed the stock market by a wide margin and the fund was eventually closed down.

Going back a few more years, another celebrated market forecaster, Joseph Granville, started his newsletter, the Granville Market Letter, in 1963. He is still an active octogenarian who continues to make market and investment forecasts. He made a few correct market calls in the 1970s and at one point was so widely followed that his predictions could move the stock market. As one might expect, accuracy was soon followed by inaccuracy in predicting the market, and his fame faded although his newsletter is still going strong, and he retains a band of loyal followers.

You might also remember two very popular books from the 1990s by Professor Ravi Batra, *The Great Depression of 1990* and *Surviving the Great Depression of 1990* in which the good professor predicted "the greatest worldwide depression in history, in which millions of people will suffer catastrophic financial reversals . . . It will occur in 1990 and plague the world through at least 1996." It turns out that the 1990s was one of the best-performing decades for stocks in history

No Free Lunch

Let's get philosophical about risk. Think about it this way: if you put money in the bank, or buy U.S. Treasury securities, you will get a return on your investment that is pretty low, say 3 percent or 4 percent today. But this investment has one important feature which is that your investment is completely safe and you can rest assured that you will get that promised return of 3 percent to 4 percent or whatever it happens to be and the return of your original investment at maturity. Okay, you say, but that level of return on my investment just isn't good enough. I need more. I need *at least* 8 percent to 10 percent on my money to achieve my financial objectives. Can I get that?

Well, yes, but with some qualifications. To get that higher return, you have to accept the possibility that you won't get an air-tight guarantee that you will get all your money back or that your 8 percent to 10 percent return is a sure thing. In other words, you have to accept risk in this investment to some degree. When you think about it, this does make sense. After all, if we could be *guaranteed* that 8 percent to 10 percent return, why would anyone invest in lower-yielding Treasury bills or put the money in the bank and get less? A guarantee is a guarantee, after all.

The answer is that to get a higher return, you have to accept the possibility that you may not get it. You have to assume some risk. And the higher return is compensation for the risk you assumed. Here again, this principle is a major tenet of modern portfolio theory. Where this gets tricky is figuring out just how much risk we should be prepared to take for the amount of return that we want. This is one of the single most important points to remember in building that winning portfolio.

Managing Risk

So now we know that we have to accept risk as part of the equation if we want to get a higher return from our portfolio. But there's some good news too. The good news is that we have learned ways we can reduce the risk we have to take. Let talk about a few of them.

The Fama/French Three-Factor Model

One of the most interesting and often overlooked studies about risk and diversification is the Fama/French three-factor model. Two finance academics, Gene Fama and Ken French, developed an interesting and important theory about risk in the stock market. In layman's language, here's what it is about.

When you invest in the stock market, you are assuming several types of risk. The first is, quite naturally, stock market risk. The stock market goes up and down and at any given time we might be making or losing money with the stocks we own. But there are other risks too as defined by Fama and French. Those risks are the ones we discussed earlier: size and style, that is, small-cap versus large-cap stocks, and growth versus value stocks. Remember that growth stocks tend to behave in the market as a group, as do value stocks and small-cap and large-cap stocks. The point here is that in addition to the risk of the market, if you have only growth stocks in your portfolio, you assume the additional risk of the one style you have chosen, that's two risks instead of one, so to speak. And it gets worse. If you have nothing but small-cap growth stocks, you add another risk, size, to the equation.

What this means is that if your portfolio consists of nothing but small-cap growth stocks, you have the following:

- Market risk
- Size risk (since you only have one size of stock, in this case, small cap)
- Style risk (since you only have one style of stock: growth)

The importance of the Fama/ French three- factor model is that it taught us that if you invest in stocks, you will inevitably have to assume market risk, but the other two risks, size and style, *can be diversified away.*

The importance of the Fama/French three-factor model is that it taught us that if you invest in stocks, you will inevitably have to assume market risk, but the other two risks, size and style, *can be diversified away*. This is major. It teaches us that we can reduce the risk in our portfolio by making sure we have both large- and small-cap stocks (which will offset the size risk) and that we have value and growth stocks (to offset the style risk). And that is precisely what we will do in building the winning portfolio.

Standard Deviation

Another measure of risk is standard deviation. Standard deviation is a statistical tool that measures volatility. In essence, it tells us, based on history, how much our portfolio might move up or down in any given time period. A low standard deviation means that your portfolio will fluctuate in a relatively small range from month to month. A high standard deviation means higher fluctuations in your portfolio. We speak of these fluctuations as degrees of risk, so standard deviation is a proxy for risk.

Put a little differently, we assume that if your portfolio is worth $100,000 and it goes up or down by $30,000, you have a very volatile portfolio and a very high standard deviation. If your portfolio only fluctuates in a typical month by $5,000, it is much less volatile and has a lower standard deviation.

Standard deviation is measured as a percentage. So if your portfolio has a standard deviation of 10 percent and your expected return is 8 percent a year, a standard deviation of 10 percent means that two-thirds of the time, your portfolio will range from –2 percent return (8 percent – 10 percent) and 18 percent on the upside (10 percent + 8 percent) for a range of returns of −2 percent to +18 percent two-thirds of the time. What happens the rest of the time, I heard you ask? The ranges get wider, but since one standard deviation covers two-thirds of the time, two standard deviations become much rarer.

If the foregoing explanation is a bit confusing, you can safely ignore it. Just remember this: A high standard deviation is riskier than a low standard deviation.

Beta

This is a stock market term you have probably heard of. Whereas standard deviation measures risk by looking at the volatility of the portfolio measured against itself, beta looks at the volatility of your entire portfolio (or even of an individual stock) measured against the volatility of the stock market as a whole. This concept is pretty simple. We use the stock market, as measured by the S&P 500, as the standard and give it a value of 1. Then we compare the volatility of your portfolio against that of the market. If your beta is 1.5, then your portfolio is 50 percent *more* volatile than the stock market. If your portfolio's beta is 0.80, then it is about 20 percent *less* volatile than the stock market.

Many investment services, like Value Line and others, as well as the large investment firms, can provide a beta for any stock you happen to own or for a mutual fund. Calculating the beta of your individual portfolio is a bit tricky, but it will consist of the weighted average of the betas of your individual holdings. As we advance toward putting together your winning portfolio, we will be attuned to the beta risk, and the portfolios I recommend will have a beta that is acceptable in terms of its volatility.

Time

One of the biggest risk investors face is time, or to put it more appropriately, patience. Remember the example of your grandparents and the $1,000 investment make in 1925? The brilliance of their investing was not that they were early Warren Buffetts or Peter Lynches. Nor did they have special stock market wisdom going for them. The single most important factor to their successful investing for their grandchildren was time. They let the markets and time take their course, and as the American economy grew, so did their investments.

So why doesn't everybody get rich in the stock market?

Answers to that important question will involve disciplines of psychology, herd mentality, anxiety, and other factors over which we have little control. Interestingly, one of the biggest factors that affect our stock market performance negatively is information. It is not that we have too little information; it is that we have too much! Compared to a couple of decades ago, the amount of financial information available to individuals today is staggering. Not only do we have entire TV networks devoted to the stock market, we also get news flashes and stock quotes streamed to our computers and even our cell phones.

What's wrong with that, you might ask? The problem is that this barrage of information induces us to action when little or no action may be the wisest and most prudent course. For example, if a company whose stock we own has a bad quarter, the financial experts and Wall Street analysts may predict gloom and doom, or downgrade the stock from a buy to a hold, or from outperform to underperform. That's usually a tip-off to sell. However, the right decision may be to recognize that any company may have a bad quarter occasionally, but if the company is sound and its business is good, the wise course may be to wait it out and continue to hold the stock.

Patience in investing is a high form of virtue. But for patience to pay off, we must have created the portfolio intelligently. Patience with a bad collection of investments will not make the bad investments better. Hence the importance of getting it right the first time. That's the difference between a winning portfolio and a losing portfolio.

Why Patience Pays Off Let's have a look at some historic time periods in the stock market. I am showing these to you to make the point about patience. Over time, stocks have risen about 10 percent a year for the past 80 years, a very good return indeed. You know, of course, that the stock market has not gone up in a straight line; that would make investing too easy. Instead, the market tends to move in fits and starts and occasionally goes through bouts of depression and anxiety.

But how bad can it get? Or put another way, how much patience might be necessary? I almost hesitate to give you this example, but I want to be sure you are familiar with the extremes, the worst-case possibilities based on history.

The chart on the following page shows the movement of the Dow Jones Average from 1966 to 1982, a 17-year period. Now we don't normally use the Dow Jones Average in discussing stock market behavior because it consists of only 30 stocks, hardly a proxy for a stock market with thousands of listings. But it is interesting to use in this example because there was lot of anticipation around the Dow Jones Average crossing the magic 1000 mark for the first time in history back in the 1960s. It came close. At the end of 1965, the Dow

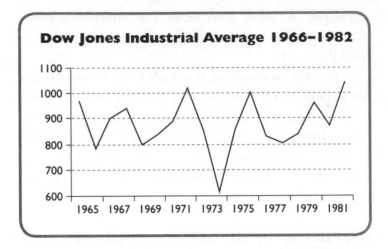

Dow Jones Industrial Average 1966–1982

Jones Average closed at 969, spitting distance from the magic 1000 mark. But it didn't quite make it that year. And if you look closely at the chart, it didn't cross the 1000 mark decisively until 17 years later, near the end of 1982!

Looking ahead, can we expect a drought of returns like this to occur again? I don't think so. But it did happen. One of the important things to remember as we build your winning portfolio is that it will not consist entirely of stocks. The portfolio will have other asset classes, and if stocks are performing poorly, there is a good chance that one or more of your other asset classes will be doing much better.

It is more reassuring to look at the historic chances for making or losing money in stocks over time. For this exercise, we have Standard & Poor's performance data going back to 1928. Take any five-year period from 1928 to 2006. Start any year you would like and ask yourself the following questions: What are the chances that I will make money in stocks over that five-year period?

The answer: 74 percent. That means that in any five-year period, you have three out of four chances, based on history, that the stock portion of your portfolio will make money.

It gets better. What are the chances of making money in the stock market in any 10-year period since 1928? Answer: 87 percent.

What are the chances of making money in the stock market in any 20-year period since 1928? Answer: 95 percent.

In fact, in my opinion, the chances of making money in stocks over these time periods is actually much better than these statistics suggest. Remember that the time period we are using starts in 1928. That includes the stock market crash in October 1929 and the Great Depression that followed in the 1930s. Perhaps you will agree that a Great Depression is an unlikely occurrence in the future given what we have learned about managing the economy over the ensuing years. That is certainly my belief.

Summing Up

The first point we need to remember is that to achieve a greater return (than a perfectly safe investment), we must assume greater risk. Our success in investing is going to be a function of how well we manage the extra risk we are taking. Over the years, a great deal of academic study, some of it rewarded with Nobel prizes, has advanced our knowledge of managing risk in the markets. All we have to do is pay attention to it. Perhaps more important, we must learn what to ignore as well as what to embrace in the search for investment knowledge. Sad to say, but no one has yet come up with a way to predict short-term stock market moves. Timing the market is a fool's errand. No one has done it successfully over an extended period of time. Or as

Peter Lynch once put it: There are no market timers in the Forbes 400.

We also discussed the concept of risk in investing. In the absence of a talent for accurately predicting the future, we rely on historic volatility to give us a clue as to how risky a particular investment might be. The idea here is that an investment class, such as small-cap growth stocks, has a historic range of returns. A wide range of historic returns means that this type of investment could be risky. A narrow range of returns shows greater stability and predictability. A winning portfolio will comprise both risky and less risky asset classes to provide the diversification we need and a higher probability of achieving the investment returns we want.

We learned early in our lives that patience is a virtue. It has never been a truer statement than when it comes to your investment portfolio. The stock market goes up most of the time; the problem is that it doesn't go up in a straight line. There are bumps and lumps along the way. We must adjust our psyches to deal with the bumps and lumps and keep our eye on the goal. A winning portfolio will get you there.

In this chapter, I also talked about the importance of diversification. The three-factor model showed us that there are some risks in the market we can diversify away. In the next chapter, on asset allocation, we will explore how to put that idea into practice.

Is Asset Allocation *Really* That Important?

Chapter 3

In 1986, Gary Brinson, a legendary money manager, and two of his colleagues, Randolph Hood and Gilbert Beebower, published a study about asset allocation. It is one of the most widely quoted—and misquoted—works to ever hit Wall Street. The basic idea was to answer the following question: If we assume that most large pension funds have the same general investment objectives, what is it that makes the performance of these funds different from one another? The study measured the investment performance of 91 large pension funds from 1973 to 1985, a nice long sample period. The study was repeated in 1991 with results similar to the original study.

The study results were quite controversial. Wall Street interpreted the results of the study to mean that 93 percent of the performance of a portfolio is attributed to the asset allocation decision. That meant that finding the smartest portfolio managers or mutual funds, timing the market, trading stocks and bonds, all that was pretty useless. In fact, doing those things might actually make your performance *worse,* rather than contribute to your success as an investor. Amazing stuff. Every young broker tucked a copy of the report under his or her arm and made the rounds expounding to clients that all you had to do was get the asset allocation right and your troubles were over.

It actually wasn't that simple. The study, in fact, did not make such a claim and it has been widely debated every since. Academics can debate whether or not the asset allocation decision accounts for 90 percent, 80 percent, or some other percentage of your portfolio's eventual performance, but we don't really care. What we do care about is the basic conclusion of the study, which is indeed correct: that the asset allocation decision is the most important decision you will make in building your winning portfolio.

Covering Your Assets

When we think about it, we have to admit that we tend to focus on what stock has the most potential or which mutual fund manager is going to emerge as the next Peter Lynch with the hot hand and sure knack for a bargain. Consider this: If the U.S. stock market is doing poorly, it isn't likely that even the best money manager is going to have a great year. Conversely, if another market, say, Japan, is having a terrific year, even a mediocre manager is going to do well. The point is that the decision of which market to favor is what will determine who has the better return in a case like this. That decision is, of course, the asset allocation decision.

The table that follows shows the percentage returns of different asset classes for three different years, 1987, 1990, and 1995.

Asset Class	1987	1990	1995
U.S. large cap (S&P 500)	5.2%	−3.2%	37.5%
EAFE-Europe	4.1	−3.4	22.1
EAFE-Japan	41.9	−36.2	0.7
U.S. small cap	−9.3	−21.5	34.5

Now imagine a bunch of different portfolios that you might create using just these four different asset classes: U.S. large-cap stocks (represented by the S&P 500 index), major European stock markets (represented by the EAFE Index-Europe), the Japanese stock market (EAFE-JAPAN) and U.S. small-cap stocks. In 1987, you had better wish that you have some allocation of your portfolio in Japan, which went up over 40 percent while the U.S. returns were in single digits or even negative (U.S. small-cap stocks). In 1990, you would have wished for just the opposite when Japan declined −36 percent. No money in Japan! Please!

Or look at the difference in the performance of the S&P 500 over those three years. In 1990, that popular index lost money. In 1995, it rose a staggering 37 percent. So you can clearly see that *where* you put your money in any of those years was far more important to your portfolio's performance than *who* was managing your money in those different markets! Indeed, if the Brinson Hood Beebower study taught us something, one of the most important lessons was that we should concentrate on the asset allocation—i.e., where we put our money and how it is divided up—and not spend much time worrying about who is managing it in these different markets. In fact, if we run out of time or patience, put it in an index fund and let the markets do the work.

Stocks are the bedrock of most portfolios. They are the best performing asset class in American history.

Getting the Allocation Right

Now that you know that asset allocation is extremely important, the next task is making sure that the chosen allocation is the right one for you. Here's where the lessons about volatility and risk come in. The right asset allocation is one that will give you the return you are seeking but with an acceptable level of risk. An aggressive asset allocation will not serve a useful purpose for you if its monthly gyrations tend to cause you to lose sleep. On the other hand, a very conservative asset allocation may take away some of your worries but may not be aggressive enough for you to achieve your financial goals.

Let's discuss some of the different asset classes that might earn a place in your winning portfolio.

Stocks

As we have already discussed, stocks are the bedrock of most portfolios. They are the best performing asset class in American history. As long as the American economy continues to grow, stocks will continue to go up. Moreover, there is a long history of price performance of stocks. We know the good and the bad, and we have learned from an extensive archive of academic studies how stocks behave in different environments.

We also have learned that different types of stocks follow different behavior patterns. This is another opportunity to reduce risk by diversifying our stocks by size (large cap and small cap) and style (value and growth).

Stocks will likely be the riskiest asset class in your portfolio. We have learned that we measure risk by volatility, using standard deviation as a measure. In assembling the winning portfolio, we will use the historic standard deviations of the stock market and even those of the specific types of stocks we choose, to create a portfolio that is well balanced among different categories of risk.

International Stocks There was a time two decades ago when the U.S. stock markets dominated world stock markets in terms of market capitalization and sheer size of trading, volume, and importance. The world has changed. The U.S. stock market is still the dominant market for securities in the world, but the rest of the world has caught up. Today, about half of the market capitalizations, or the market values of the different stocks, is located outside of the United States. A winning portfolio will have representation in many international markets in addition to U.S. markets. International stocks are generally considered somewhat riskier than U.S. stocks. Also, although international markets have improved greatly, especially in developed countries, no markets are better regulated worldwide than the markets in the United States. These are other risk elements we must consider.

Emerging Markets This is likely to be the single riskiest asset class in anyone's portfolio. Stocks in this category are in markets that are relatively new to securities trading and do not have decades of history and regulation as do the established stock markets. Examples of emerging markets include giant countries like India and China, and also much smaller ones like Egypt, Turkey, and Thailand. The history of emerging market is one of dizzying fluctuations.

Fixed Income

This category consists of bonds, either U.S. government securities, or corporate securities. It may even include preferred stock and CDs, basically anything with a fixed rate of return.

Years ago, bank trust department officers in three-piece suits would welcome clients into their wood paneled offices and prepared what we call 60 – 40 portfolios for them. That means that 60 percent of the portfolio was invested in stocks, usually blue chips of the day such as General Motors, U.S. Steel, Sperry Rand, ALCOA, among others. The rest of the portfolio, the 40 percent part, was invested in high-quality bonds, both government and corporate.

In those days, bond yields were quite attractive. The fixed-income portion of the portfolio would throw off a return of perhaps 6 percent or 7 percent. Of course, this was during a time when interest rates were higher than they are today. If you are old enough, perhaps you remember the severe period of inflation in the U.S. in the late 1970s. The prime rate at banks, the rate that banks charge for loans to their best customers, rose to an astounding 21½ percent in 1980. The U.S. Treasury issued long-term bonds at an interest rate of 14 percent, which sounds almost incredible today. But it did happen.

Throughout the 1980s, interest rates began a slow, steady decline, reaching a point in early 2005 when the discount rate was a paltry 1 percent. Interest rates have gone up since then but are still close to historic lows in mid-2007. As a result, bond yields are also quite low. In the "old days," the fixed-income portion of the 60 – 40 portfolio, the 40 percent part, was not very exciting but it still offered a decent yield, anywhere from 5 percent to 8 percent with little risk. Much of the bond portion of the portfolio was invested in government securities and also in top-rated corporate debt.

CORPORATE BOND RATINGS

There are three agencies who rate the credit of corporate bonds. They are: Standard & Poor's, Moody's, and Fitch IBCA.

These agencies analyze the companies issuing the debt and determine a rating based on their evaluation of the risk involved in investing in the bonds of these companies. In other words, what are your chances of getting your money back when the bonds mature?

The agencies use slightly different scoring mechanisms, but for all of them, the highest rating is AAA, then comes AA, followed by A, then BBB, and so on. Another breakpoint for these ratings is the determination of "investment grade." Investment Grade is a designation used by many institutions to determine if an investment qualifies as a high-quality investment. Some institutions, like banks, are not allowed to invest in bonds below investment grade. Typically, investment grade bonds are those rated BBB and higher. Below that level, the noninvestment grade bonds are commonly referred to as "junk" bonds.

All that has changed. For one thing, there is precious little highly rated corporate debt left. Back in 1983, 32 nonfinancial (excluding banks and insurance companies and the like) companies held the coveted AAA designation, the Olympic gold medal of the bond rating industry. Today (mid-2007) the AAA rating is held by only seven American companies.

You will no doubt want to know who the AAA companies are. Here's the list: Automatic Data Processing, Berkshire Hathaway (which is considered a financial company), ExxonMobil, General Electric, Johnson & Johnson, Pfizer, and United Parcel Service.

So there is not a lot of high-quality corporate debt to choose from today. As a result, the fixed-income portion of most contemporary portfolios consists mostly of U.S. government securities. And since the yield on these securities is quite low, around 4 percent or a little higher, this part of the portfolio tends to be a drag on performance. But it serves another useful purpose in the process. The bond portion of the portfolio acts as ballast against stormy weather in the stock market. The bond allocation tends to have a very low standard deviation, so it is unlikely to fluctuate widely and therefore unlikely to negatively affect the portfolio during times of stock market turbulence.

But to many investors, the fact that the bond portion of the portfolio is a drag on performance, particularly during times when the other asset classes are doing well, is an irritant. It is something that needs to be addressed.

Generally speaking, most investment advisors trim the bond (fixed-income) portion of portfolios depending on the age, risk tolerance, and time objectives of their clients. There's a good reason for doing this. Remember that the stock market goes up most of the time. The examples we gave earlier about the 5-, 10-, and 20-year time periods show that as you lengthen the holding period of your stock market investments, you greatly increase the chances that you will make money. If we start the series of stock market performance statistics after the Great Depression in the 1930s, the odds get even better. Indeed, if we start the series in the 1940s, there are no examples of 20-year periods when you lost money in stocks, no matter what year you started. So it makes sense that if your time horizon is long, and you otherwise qualify for the risk of stocks, a higher allocation to stocks will be justified and you will have more money working for you and earning a higher return than is available today in the bond market. As a result, when we get to the portion of the book that deals with putting together your personal winning portfolio, we will take into account the amount of equities and bonds, and corresponding risk, that is appropriate for you.

Commodities

In the old days, commodities had no place in most investment portfolios. They were considered too risky, and frankly, most investment advisors didn't understand them at all. After all, who wanted to understand, much less own, pork bellies?

Today, we need to take a look at some commodities that might have a place in any winning portfolio. We are not generally considering the usual farm commodities of wheat, corn, and the proverbial pork bellies. Instead, in this category we are looking for inflation hedges and noncorrelating assets. Noncorrelating assets? That's our fancy expression for investments that don't correlate well with one another or whose performance doesn't parallel another type of investment. We'll discuss this more fully later on because it is an important concept you must retain.

The kind of commodities that we are seeking will offer protection against inflation and also participation in a commodity that may have other reasons besides inflation to do well. Some investment advisors call this part of the portfolio *Inflation Hedge*.

I want to concentrate on two commodities for your portfolio: gold and energy.

Gold Gold has a sterling past as an investment (forgive me, I couldn't resist!). In the inflation plagued years of the 1970s, gold rose to vertiginous heights, peaking at $850 an ounce in January 1980. Silver had a comparable performance, peaking at a price of $48 per ounce in early 1980.

Around that time people were taking everything in silver and gold in their homes that wasn't nailed down and rushing to the smelter to sell it. That was a good decision at the time. Over the next 20 years, gold sank from the high of $850 an ounce to around $250 in July 1999. Silver crashed from $48 at the beginning of 1980 to a low of $5 in June 1982.

More recently, gold has enjoyed another revival, climbing from the 1999 low of about $250 to over $650 in mid-2007. Investors have taken a fresh look at gold and seen some value in its future as well as in its diversification benefit in a portfolio.

Gold remains an almost pure inflation hedge. When inflation scares abound, gold tends to do well. It is also the commodity of choice whenever global fears run rampant through any part of the world. Wars, uprisings, natural disasters, currency collapses, hedge fund blow-ups—all of these disasters cause an immediate and even Pavlovian flight to gold.

Gold also tends to rise with inflation. In fact, gold's major rise in the 1970s was largely due to the serious inflation plague the world suffered at that time. It becomes clear how gold can act as a very useful part of a diversified portfolio. Speaking of noncorrelating asset classes, gold is as pure a noncorrelating choice as you can find. When the world is worried about everything there is to worry about, the world's investment attention immediately turns to gold.

There is, of course, another side to this story. Here again, when the rest of your portfolio is humming along, gold will likely not be contributing to your wealth at all. Remember that gold thrives at times of crises. No crisis, no action in gold. So if gold is going to be a part of your winning portfolio, consider it the same way you consider an insurance policy. You pay the premiums, and you hope the money is wasted since the last thing you want to do is have a catastrophe that will force you to collect on your insurance policy.

Energy Given the importance of energy to the world, investments in energy *should* be an appropriate consideration for the winning portfolio. Given normal economic growth, plus the extraordinary growth from China and India, demand for energy is soaring. And the ability to produce the oil needed is under considerably more pressure than ever before. Consider the chart on the following page and the trends in capacity.

The World Energy Resources Program of the U.S. Geological Survey, which produces the official estimates of world oil resources for the U.S. federal government, estimates the remaining world oil reserves at about 1 trillion (1,000 billion) barrels. If correct, that would mean world oil reserves would be exhausted in 50 to 100 years at the current rate of consumption. The world consumes over 85 million barrels of oil each day, and by 2005, the spare capacity to produce oil dropped to less than 1 million barrels per day—just 1 percent of world oil demand. One cannot help but be struck by Exxon-Mobil former chairman Lee Raymond's stark prediction that by 2020—a date not that far off in the future—we will require the additional energy equivalent to eight Saudi Arabias, the world's largest producer of oil.

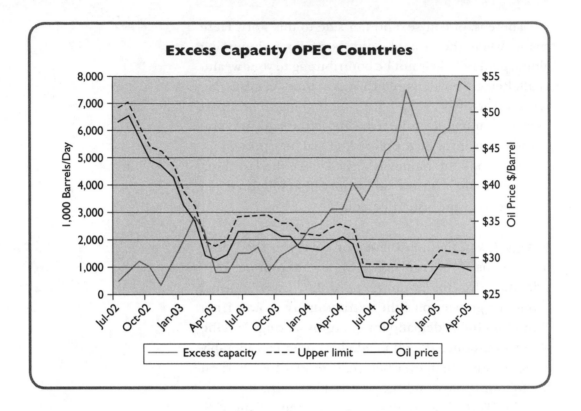

Excess Capacity OPEC Countries

There are a number of potential alternative sources of energy, but even the most simple analysis suggests that most of our energy will continue to come from fossil fuels for decades to come. Corn ethanol arguably requires more energy to produce than it generates: if we were to replace just 10 percent of the gasoline the world will use in 2020 with corn-based ethanol, we would need to plant an area equivalent to Illinois, Indiana, and Ohio solely to grow the corn needed for ethanol production. Similarly, solar and wind power are expensive alternatives and are subject to limitations of location and size, among others, that also make them expensive. Hydrogen offers some promise, but until a more efficient hydrogen-based energy fuel cell can be developed, there is no practical or economic way for it to power cars and other vehicles.

So while there is considerable debate about just how many years of oil we have left, two basic facts are true: There is a finite amount of oil in the world, and unless new cost-effective fuels are developed, the world will run out of oil—at least *cheap* oil. So what does this mean for your portfolio? The upward movement of the price of oil means an increase in the value of the oil-related investments; this will help offset losses in other parts of your portfolio. And that last statement is a very good way to introduce the next topic.

> **In a diversified, winning portfolio we want noncorrelating investments that all do well over time, but not at the same time.**

Noncorrelating Asset Classes

The reason we pay attention to this is another part of true diversification. I mentioned earlier that owning five large-cap growth mutual funds will not give you a diversified portfolio because those growth mutual funds will tend to have similar behavior characteristics. That means that when one of your funds is going up, they'll all be going up, and when one of them is going down, they'll all be going down. Obviously, that's not a diversified portfolio.

Important rule: In a diversified, winning portfolio we want noncorrelating investments that all do well over time, but not at the same time. This will even out the performance and prevent roller coaster episodes of up and down investment results.

Here's how correlation works from a statistical point of view. We determine correlation by a range of values from +1 to −1. A value of +1 means perfect correlation. What that means is that if you have, say, two stocks, A and B, and stock A goes up 10 percent, stock B also goes up 10 percent. So anything less than +1 means that the two stocks are not perfectly correlated. Of course, if their correlation value is .90, well, they aren't perfectly correlated, but they are *very* correlated—90 percent correlated, as a matter of fact. So if +1 is perfectly correlated and a value of less than 1 means not perfectly correlated, what if the correlation is –1? That means the opposite of perfectly correlated—perfectly noncorrelated. That would give us the following scenario: stock A goes up 10 percent. Okay, what does stock B do? Well, if it is perfectly *negatively* correlated, when stock A goes up 10 percent stock B goes *down* 10 percent! And a value of 0 means not correlated at all. If stock A goes up, stock B will do something different. We're not sure what, but it will have no specific relationship to what stock A does most of the time.

I think you get the idea. To determine the correlation value of different types of investments, statisticians and investment advisors have to develop a correlation matrix. The chart below is a typical correlation matrix, the kind most investment advisors can prepare.

Typical Correlation Matrix

	Correlation with Cash	Correlation with Large Cap	Correlation with Small Cap	Correlation with EAFE	Correlation with LB Aggregate Bond	Correlation with Gold Future	Correlation with Crude Oil Future
Cash	1.00	–0.04	–0.04	–0.07	0.08	–0.06	0.00
Large Cap	–0.04	1.00	0.68	0.46	0.21	–0.01	–0.15
Small Cap	–0.04	0.68	1.00	0.52	0.14	0.17	–0.08
MSCI EAFE	–0.07	0.46	0.52	1.00	0.15	0.23	–0.04
LB Aggregate Bond	0.08	0.21	0.14	0.15	1.00	0.08	–0.07
Gold Future	–0.06	–0.01	0.17	0.23	0.08	1.00	0.25
Crude Oil Futures	0.00	–0.15	–0.08	–0.04	–0.07	0.25	1.00

For example, large-cap stocks have a low correlation to MSCI EAFE—a broad index of foreign stocks—at 0.46, which tells you that adding foreign stocks to your portfolio is a good diversification move. At –0.25, crude oil has a negative correlation to large-cap stocks, another good diversifying asset. Of course, you won't actually buy oil, but you might own some oil stocks or a low-cost diversified energy fund such as the Vanguard Energy Fund. A glance at some of these correlations demonstrates the value of picking asset classes and investments that don't all move in the same direction at the same time.

Hedge Funds

Yes, hedge funds can be scary! But what are they? These investment vehicles are structured as partnerships. The general partner (or GP) is the fellow or team running the fund. The limited partners are the investors who put up the money for the managers to invest. Hedge funds are different from most other investments in several ways. First, they can do a lot of different things that an ordinary money manager or mutual fund can't do. They can "go short," which is selling a stock you don't own to make money when the stock goes down.

Some hedge funds use leverage—that is, they borrow money to leverage the investment. Hedge funds may also use derivatives, a broad term used to describe financial instruments like options, which allow investors to buy or sell a stock or commodity at a fixed price some time in the future. Finally, hedge funds require a marriage of sorts with their investors. Most of them require that you stay invested for at least a year to start, and thereafter you can only get out at three- or six-month intervals. So liquidity is poor and if you need your money in a hurry, you are out of luck.

All of this leverage makes these investments risky. If the manager is successful, the limited partners make a lot of money and the general partner makes a lot of money, too. Hedge funds also differ from mutual funds in how the managers are compensated. Hedge fund

SHORT SELLING

When you sell short, you sell stock you don't actually own. In order to deliver the stock you sold to the buyer, you have to borrow an equivalent amount of shares to make good on your sale. You sell stock short because you think the price is going down. Here's an example:

You think ABC stock is going down. It is selling at 50 and you think it is highly overvalued. You decide to sell 100 shares short at $50 a share for total proceeds of $5,000. (I'm ignoring the commission costs in this example.) Your broker arranges to borrow 100 shares of ABC to deliver to the buyer of the stock you sold since he doesn't know or care that you sold short when he bought it from you. He expects to get the stock he bought.

Since your judgment is impeccable, ABC tumbles down to $10 a share and you decide you made enough money so you buy back 100 shares of ABC at $10 a share for a total cost of $1,000. You then deliver the stock you just bought to the firm that lent you the 100 shares of ABC in the first place. But look what happened: You got $5,000 when you sold the stock at $50 a share and it only cost you $1,000 when you bought it back, so you made a profit of $5,000 minus $1,000 to buy it back or $4,000. Good work.

A quick word of caution: If you are wrong about the short sale and the stock goes up instead of down, your losses can be dramatic. You have to buy it back some day to repay the stock you borrowed. So if it goes up a lot, your losses are potentially unlimited. Short selling is not for the faint of heart—or pocketbook.

managers usually earn a 1 percent or 2 percent fee on the assets they manage plus a percentage of the profits, typically 20 percent, known as the *incentive fee*. Given this type of fee structure, it is no surprise that many mutual fund managers would rather trade in their 0.75 percent to 1.25 percent fee with no incentive compensation for the rich rewards of running a hedge fund.

Should You Own Hedge Funds? Possibly. But I never recommend that an individual own one or even two hedge funds. The risk is too great, no matter how clever or successful the manager. Let me give you one example of that: A very successful hedge fund called Amaranth Advisors laid a nasty surprise on its investors in September 2006. A 32-year-old hotshot trader took a big bet on natural gas, and bet wrong. The result: The fund lost a staggering $6 billion in a few days, more than half the value of the fund. Was this loss predictable? No. Did the smart money know better and stay away? No. Those very smart people at Goldman Sachs have a hedge fund of funds called Global Alpha, which was invested in Amaranth and the fund of funds lost 10 percent of its value. The point is that there is no way to mitigate the risk, however rare it might be, in owning a hedge fund . . . except one: Buy a fund of funds. These are the equivalent of mutual funds except that instead of owning stocks, they own hedge funds. In so doing, they diversify the risk of owning a single fund by owning dozens of them. Most also use the principles of noncorrelation to ensure that they are not victims of a single strategy that falls on hard times.

Most investors, however, are unlikely to own hedge funds or even funds of funds. Even if you ignore my advice and seek out individual hedge funds, most have minimum investment requirements of $1 million and the SEC has rules as to how wealthy an investor must be to qualify to own them. Funds of funds have similar restrictions although there are a few funds of hedge funds that accept smaller investment amounts. In general, however, unless your portfolio is $10 million or larger, I would stay away from hedge funds.

Options

Options are the right to buy or sell a security at a specific price for a specific amount of time. Speculators use them to bet on the price move of a stock or even the market as a whole. Let's say you feel very strongly that Acme Widgets is about to soar. You use one of their widgets at home and it is just about the best gadget you have ever come across. You are convinced that this gadget is about to become a major sensation and sweep the country. You look up the stock and it trades around $40 a share. If you invest $4,000 you can buy 100 shares. But you feel like doing something riskier to possibly make a small killing. You look to see if there are any options on Acme and, sure enough, there is a market on the American Stock Exchange in the *puts* and *calls* of Acme Widgets. Calls give you the right to buy the stock at a fixed price for a fixed amount of time. Puts give you the right to sell the stock at a fixed price for a fixed amount of time.

You find that there are calls at different strike prices and with different expiration dates. The *strike price* is the price you can buy the stock at, and the *expiration date* is the last day on which you can exercise your right to buy the stock at that fixed price. *In the money* calls are those that can be exercised right away at a profit. So if the stock is selling at $40, any call option to buy the stock at $40 or less is considered in the money. *Out of the money* calls are those whose exercise price is higher than the current price. Logical, right? So if you have a call option to buy the stock at $40, and the stock is selling at $30, that option isn't worth a whole lot. After all, why would you use an option to buy a stock at $40 if you can just buy it on the stock market for its current price of $30?

Now if you are speculating on a big move in Acme Widgets, you might want to buy the out of the money options. Here's an example: You find call options on Acme with an exercise price of $50 that expire in six months. Since the stock currently sells for $40, those call options are severely out of the money; the stock has to go up another $10 for the options to be worth anything. Since the options are out of the money, they only trade for, say, $4. So with $400, you'd have the right to buy 100 shares of Acme at $50 a share over the next six months. If you want to gamble $4,000, you could buy 10 options (100 shares each) at $50 a share instead of the current $40. Now assume that the stock goes to $60. You will then have a profit of at least $10 a share since you can buy the stock at $50 and sell it at $60. And your 10 options give you the right to buy 1,000 shares, so this becomes real money, a profit of $10,000 on your investment of $4,000.

Before anyone gets excited about buying options, let's look at the other possibility. Suppose Acme goes down or doesn't move for six months. The stock stays at $40. Well, your call option to buy the stock at $50 is worthless. And after six months your options expire—worthless. You lose the $4,000 you invested. So it is clear that you can make a lot of money with options if you are lucky, and you can lose your entire investment if you are not lucky.

Writing Options Writing options is another matter. Suppose you *own* Acme Widgets and you aren't really sure the stock is going to go up a lot more than $40. You could sell out of the money calls to someone who wants to speculate on a price move. The speculator pays you $4 a share, just like in the previous example. Here's where that leaves you:

- If Acme stays around $40 for the next six months or stays under $50, the option you sold expires worthless and you keep the $4. Maybe you could sell another option for $4 to another sucker—sorry, investor—who wants to speculate on the price going up.

- If Acme goes down, you still get to keep the $4 a share.
- If Acme goes up to, say, $60 the stock will be "called away" from you and you will have effectively sold it for $50 plus the $4 you got for the option. You won't get the current price of $60, but you likely won't be too unhappy about that.

Now you know about options and how they work, but in my experience, most investors who buy options lose money. As you can see from the above example, if you are going to do any options trading, I recommend that you sell options on your existing holdings, not buy them.

Summing Up

In this chapter, we have discussed the importance of asset allocation. The simple fact is that where you put your money—in what kinds of stocks, bonds, or commodities and in what percentage of each—is likely the single most important decision you will make in building your winning portfolio. We also discussed the importance of correlation and the desirability of choosing noncorrelating asset classes in putting your portfolio together.

We covered most of the different types of investments you might want to consider, including some that I don't think you should consider at all, but which you should know about anyway.

Finally, I realize I have laid a lot of information on you in this chapter. You might want to take a break and let it all sink in. Then we'll move on to an interesting discussion of the efficient market theory.

The Efficient Market Theory

We mentioned that there are two types of investing, active and passive. Active investing is the process by which you, or a professional investment manager or mutual fund manager, picks stocks and builds a portfolio. If you, or an investment professional, pick your own stocks, what is your objective? The answer is simple. You are buying stocks and investing actively because you don't want to get the stock market's return, you want to *beat* it.

Welcome to the Efficient Market Theory

The efficient market theory, EMT for short, has been studied by countless finance academics, including many Nobel Prize recipients in economics. I authored an entire book on this subject (*Investment Gurus*, Prentice Hall, 1997) in which I interviewed active managers like Peter Lynch, Mario Gabelli, and Foster Friess, as well as noted finance academics including two Nobel Prize winners, Bill Sharpe and Merton Miller.

So what's the fuss about? Simply this: The academic community generally believes that stock markets are efficient. Efficiency in this case is defined as a state in which all publicly known information about a company is instantly reflected in the price of the company's stock. So if a company is doing well, all of the good news publicly available about that company is now reflected in the price of the stock at any given time.

I know that doesn't sound very dramatic. But before you say "So what?" think about the consequences of this statement. If stocks are priced efficiently, as they say, what purpose do research reports, stockbrokers, market commentators, and prognosticators serve? If everything that is known about a company is already in the stock price, what do these research papers and stock recommendations add? In the minds of the efficient market theorists, the answer is nothing. To them, writing a report that concludes that ABC stock is a "good buy at current levels," is just blather because the writer can't possibly know what the future holds. To belabor the point, the EMT crowd will say that any good news that particular research analyst knows is already in the stock price.

You might ask, if this is true, then what will make the stock price go up or down in the future? The answer is new information. As subsequent news comes out about the company, the stock price will adjust to the latest news by going up or down, depending on whether or not the news is good or bad.

You can see how the consequences of this debate become enormous. Indeed, if stocks are priced efficiently, then all of the money spent on research on stocks, the billions of dollars invested by Wall Street in promoting stocks because the research department thinks they are good buys, is simply guesswork. It comes as no surprise that Wall Street is not a big proponent of the efficient market theory.

Investment Gurus

The theory also seems to ignore the fact that there are many examples of money managers who do, in fact, beat the stock market. To cite but two of the more famous names, we have already talked about Peter Lynch who managed the Fidelity Magellan Fund for 13 years and has an astounding record of 29 percent a year annualized during the period he ran the fund. That was far better than the stock market's return. There is also Warren Buffett's legendary record. Do they not disprove the contention that you can't beat the market through intelligent research and stock selection?

In the interview I did in *Investment Gurus* with Rex Sinquefield, who was then (but has since retired) chairman of DFA, a large California-based manager of index type funds. I asked if there wasn't enough evidence that some people can beat the market.

Here's part of his answer: "Your question is, basically, are there some people who can systematically see the future. That's what it comes down to . . . . Do you think it is credible that there is one person who systematically has more information than a dispersed market of 6 billion people? That's not remotely credible. But that's the condition that somebody has to prove."

Tough talk. It still doesn't answer the question about a known fact: Some managers do beat the market, so how do you explain that in the context of the efficient market theory? Simple, say the EMT proponents. They are "outliers."

Now if you haven't spent a lot of your academic or spare time studying statistics, the term *outlier* may not be very familiar to you. So let me bring you up to speed simply and efficiently. In statistics, there is the concept of the normal distribution curve, or bell curve.

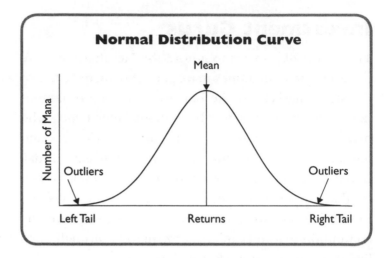

Let's assume that this distribution curve represents the performance of a few thousand money managers and mutual funds over a period of time. In the fat part of the bell-shaped curve, you will have the bulk of the returns. The mean return is likely to be the stock market's return. Most managers' returns are somewhere around this number. To the extreme right and left of the curve are the outliers. On the right tail, you will find the money managers or mutual fund managers who beat the market by a wide margin. On the left tail, you'll see the outliers who underperformed the market by a wide margin and will likely never be heard from again.

Of course, we tend to concentrate on the right-tail outliers, the ones who decisively beat the market, the Peter Lynches and Warren Buffetts, if you will. To the EMT folks, they show up as great managers as part of a normal distribution. The point made by the efficient market theorists is that these outliers can't be predicted. In fact, in most cases, studies of top-performing mutual funds over a period of time indicate that the majority of them don't repeat their past success. For example, if you buy a mutual fund based on its great five-year record, there is likely not more than a 50/50 chance that the fund will repeat its superb record over the next five years.

The EMT folks will also concede that there is the occasional Warren Buffett or Peter Lynch or some other amazing guru who will defy all odds and beat the market for a long period of time. To them, they are the extreme outliers. They will also point out that if you let a thousand monkeys bang away at a thousand typewriters for a thousand years, one of them will end up writing *Romeo and Juliet* by chance.

So Can You Beat the Market or Not?

There you have it. What do you think about the efficient market theory? Do you think you can beat the market? Or do you believe that the most prudent course of action is to buy a group of index funds and achieve your portfolio diversification that way, with lower costs and assurance that you may not beat the market, but you won't do any worse than the market either.

To me, the answer lies in a little bit of both. Take a look at the chart on the following page.

This chart represents the 15-year returns (1992–2006) of the 349 mutual funds in the Morningstar database that are large-cap funds benchmarked against the S&P 500 Index. The question you want answered is this: how many of these funds beat the S&P 500 over that 15-year period? Not many. Look at the bar entitled "S&P 500 Index" on the chart and you will see that it comes in right around fund number 120. That means that only about one-third of the actively managed funds beat the index over the 15-year period. In other words, if you bought one of these mutual funds 15 years ago,

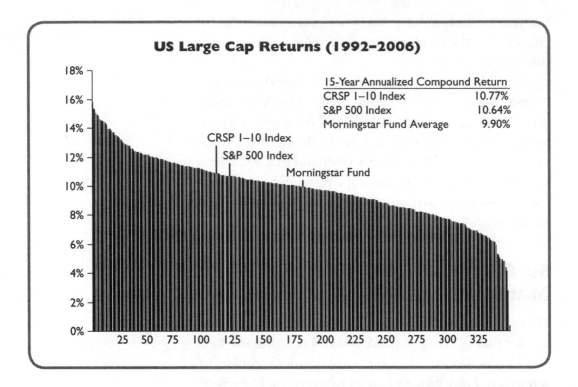

US Large Cap Returns (1992–2006)

15-Year Annualized Compound Return	
CRSP 1–10 Index	10.77%
S&P 500 Index	10.64%
Morningstar Fund Average	9.90%

CRSP 1–10 Index

S&P 500 Index

Morningstar Fund

you had about a one in three chance to beat the market performance you would have gotten by buying an S&P 500 Index fund instead.

Moreover, for that bet on large-cap actively managed funds to really pay off, you would have had to pick one of the top 25 or so funds that outperformed the market by a significant amount. (Take a look at the bulge on the far left side of the chart, roughly the top 25 performing funds, to see what I mean.) You would have had to have been very lucky to pick one of the top 25 funds out of the 349 in this sample.

Let me add that similar analyses in the Morningstar database covering mutual fund performance for 5 and 10 years also show that less than half of the actively managed large-cap funds beat the S&P 500 over their respective 5- and 10-year time periods.

As you have just seen, over half the investment professionals can't beat the market consistently. Now to be sure, they have an additional handicap—they charge fees! The stock market doesn't charge fees. So when you compare the performance of the managers against the performance of the stock market, just to stay even, the managers have to make up the fees they charge their clients. If an average equity fund charges 1.5 percent in annual expenses, then they have to earn 1.5 percent more than the market for their investors to be even. Yes, there are fees involved in owning an index fund, but a typical S&P 500 Index fund will charge between 0.10 percent and 0.20 percent, or about one-tenth the fees charged by the active managers.

So what's an investor to do? You can find many different answers to that question. I'll give you mine. After writing an entire book on the subject and interviewing both active managers and finance academics, including two Nobel Prize winners, I concluded that the market is indeed efficient, but not as perfectly efficient as the academic community would have you believe. Indeed, experience suggests that information about a company is not instantaneously reflected in the stock price. It takes time for that information to get around. That means that a sharp analyst who gets and analyzes some information before others will have an edge, and perhaps better stock market performance too.

This assumption also leads to another conclusion. If there are **many** analysts following a particular company, it is unlikely that one will have a major advantage over another one since they will all be on top of every piece of information that comes out about the companies they follow. This in turn leads us to believe that it is particularly hard to get an edge covering the most widely followed stocks, which are generally the largest companies. For example, there are dozens of analysts on Wall Street and across the country who follow companies like Microsoft, Google, and Apple, all large companies with a wide following. Every word coming out of these companies is instantly scrutinized not only by these analysts, but also by thousands of interested investors. It isn't surprising then to assume that any information about these well-followed companies will be reflected almost instantaneously in the price of the companies' stock. That makes for an efficient market.

If market efficiency applies to large, well-known companies, what about the others? Smaller companies, or less-followed larger companies, don't get the scrutiny that the larger companies get. Therefore, information that comes out about these companies is less likely to be instantaneously reflected in their stock prices. A sharp analyst or investor may find out something and beat everyone to the punch by putting out a recommendation or, in the case of an investor, by buying the stock.

Summing Up

Our most pressing question is this: What does all this mean in putting together a winning portfolio? Let's take another look at the chart showing the performance of mutual funds against the S&P 500. What these funds have in common is that they all invest in large company stocks. So if large company stocks are generally priced efficiently, what should we do? We should buy an index fund instead for this part of our winning portfolio. Here's the logic:

- Large-cap stocks are priced efficiently.
- Most large-cap mutual funds *do not* beat the market over time.

■ Actively managed mutual funds charge much higher fees than index funds.

Therefore, we should buy index funds for that portion of our portfolio that will be dedicated to large company stocks. In so doing, we will not take the chance that the active mutual fund we might have picked will underperform the market. And we will save money on the fees, since index funds charge much lower fees than actively managed mutual funds.

Of course, if you still want to pick an actively managed large-cap mutual fund, you can always do that. When we talk about the actual portfolios you can create, there will be an allocation to large-cap stocks. I will recommend that you use passive (index) funds for this part of your portfolio, but if you feel strongly that you or your adviser can pick a large-cap mutual fund that will beat the market, feel free to disagree with me.

Mutual Funds: The Cornerstone of Your Winning Portfolio

Chapter 5

In the preceding chapters we have talked about the many different kinds of investments you might want to have in your winning portfolio. We also discussed the risk characteristics of the various investments and the importance of diversification. We talked about the important decision you will need to make about active versus passive investing—that is, whether you will pick investments that match market returns or some that you hope will beat the market.

The title of this chapter says that mutual funds are going to be the cornerstone of your winning portfolio. But why mutual funds? Why not just buy stocks? Wall Street firms, and their thousands of stockbrokers, thrive on stock recommendations from their highly paid research analysts. The investment community lives off recommendations of what stocks to recommend that its customers buy. We're talking about a very big industry with one purpose: to get you in the game, to get you to buy and sell stocks for fun and profit.

I hope you have been convinced so far that while it may be possible to beat the market, it is very difficult to do so consistently. You saw in the preceding chapter that the majority of the professional mutual fund managers do not beat the stock market over long periods of time.

So I have to ask you a very important question. Just think about it and answer it as candidly as you can. Please explain to me, and more important, to yourself, how you are going to do better than the professional money managers who do this 8 or 10 hours a day, when you only spend a few minutes, maybe an hour tops? Now I am assuming you are just as smart as they are. But you might concede that they have more background and training in analyzing stocks than you do, and they will spend far more work time doing it than you will. I'm sure you can see how you might not be able to perform better than they do.

Does that mean that you shouldn't pick stocks? Not necessarily. In my four decades of experience, I have found that there are some talented nonprofessional stock pickers out there, and you might well be one of them. These successful investors can be found in all professions—doctors, bus drivers, lawyers, and mechanics. But they all share that singular passion; they love to pick stocks. So they do their research, read the financial pages every day, watch CNBC, and subscribe to a bunch of great magazines like *Kiplinger's, Smart Money, Money, Forbes,* and others. These dedicated investors spend a great deal of time on their passion, and they do it because to them it is fun, not work. If you are one of these people, by all means, spend some time and money picking stocks for your winning portfolio.

But don't do all of the work yourself. Trust most of it to professionals. Who are these professionals? They are the folks who run the thousands of mutual funds you will choose from. Speaking for myself, there are some activities where I insist on being served by a professional, not an amateur. Surgery is one of them. Flying

WHERE HAVE ALL THE STOCKBROKERS GONE?

When I grew up in the business in the 1960s, being a stockbroker with a major firm like Merrill Lynch, Bache, or Dean Witter was a respected and much aspired-to profession if you were interested in finance or the stock market. Over the years, the profession has fallen on some degree of ill repute through various scandals and accusations of churning (the practice of turning over portfolios by buying and selling securities in order to generate commission income) aggressive sales tactics, trading on inside information, and other unsavory practices. How the world has changed! Today, there are still countless stockbrokers but they go by different names. They are "financial consultants," "investment consultants," financial advisors," and so forth. In some cases, the changes are real; in others it is simply a case of changing the title to make it look more respectable.

There is an old saying that stocks are sold, not bought. And to sell stocks, or anything else, you need salesmen. The problem is that salespeople who are successful are those who sell the most. That fact might not be in your best interests as an investor. So whenever you get the business card of someone in the financial services industry, look beyond the title. More on this later in chapter 9.

an airplane is another; I don't fly with amateur pilots. And the business of managing a portfolio is the same.

Load versus No-Load

We discussed earlier the types of mutual funds, load and no-load. Load funds are primarily sold by securities salesman, since an important part of their compensation comes from commissions they earn on the sale of various financial products, including mutual funds. The problem here is that this practice does not align your interests with the interests of the securities salesman. You are interested in getting the best mutual funds you can at the lowest cost. The salesman is also interested in getting you the best mutual funds, but preferably ones that include fat compensation for him.

Mutual Fund Fees

There is very little reason, if any at all, to buy a load fund—one that includes a commission for the salesman that comes out of your pocket. I have no objection to fees if you get something for the fee you are paying. For example, if most of the better managed and better performing mutual funds were those that came with a sales charge, or load, I would be happy to consider these funds in any portfolio. But that is simply not the case. So why do these load funds exist? Because securities are sold, not bought. Never underestimate the power of a good sales pitch!

The Investment Company Institute, a funds industry trade group, estimated that over half of the mutual fund buyers did not pay attention to the fees and expenses of the funds they were considering. That, my friends, is sad.

In recent years, financial journalists began to hammer away at the importance of paying attention to fees, and those articles and reports started to have some effect on the mutual fund industry. So what did the mutual fund industry titans do? Lower fees? Of course not! They just engaged in a creative whirlwind of masterful obfuscation by making the fee structure more complicated. Now if a securities salesman (sorry, financial advisor) wants to sell you a load fund and you ask what the sales charge is, he might answer that the sales charge on the Class A shares of the fund is 5.5 percent. But you read all about those load charges, so you immediately object and tell him you don't want to pay that sales charge since it comes out of your investment. No problem, says the salesman, we can get you the same fund with no sales charge. These are the Class B shares, especially designed for the true cognoscenti like you.

Class B shares have no upfront sales charge. Whew! That's a relief. Unfortunately, there are other charges you will pay called, appropriately enough, *deferred sales charges*. This can be as high as 4 percent the first year, and 1 percent for a few years thereafter. Then there are also other sneaky charges called 12b-1 fees that can add another 1 percent annually which comes out of your investment each and every year. This makes a fund with a 1.5 percent expense ratio really cost 2.5 percent. Remember, we saw just how hard it was to beat the stock market. With heavy fees, the job becomes that much harder. Sadly, few people can afford the time and energy to go through and untangle this maze of fees. The answer: stick with no-load funds. That's all we'll talk about from now on. And we'll tell you where and how to find them.

Active versus Passive

The first decision in selecting funds is the active versus passive fund decision. Active funds are run by professional fund managers who try to beat the stock market performance. Passive funds match the stock market performance and are a lot cheaper than active funds since they don't require highly paid money managers to make decisions.

There are lots of passive funds. The Vanguard 500 Index Fund—the best known index—tracks the S&P 500. This is also one of the largest mutual funds, with $70 billion in assets. It's the fund of choice for that part of the portfolio that is chosen to give pure stock market returns. The cost, or expense ratio, of this fund is only

0.18 percent. The Vanguard 500 Index Fund isn't the only index fund that Vanguard manages. In fact, the company manages dozens of them including "style specific" funds, such as a fund specializing in growth stocks and one specializing in value stocks.

Vanguard manages active funds too. And without beating you over the head with this point, I am amused that even some of Vanguard's own active funds find it hard to beat their passive counterparts. The U.S. Value Fund is actively managed and has an expense ratio of 0.39 percent, quite reasonable for an actively managed fund. (The passive fund's cost is 0.21 percent.) For a five-year period ending in early 2007, the U.S. Value Fund had annualized performance of 8.52 percent. The Value Index Fund, passively managed, had annualized performance over the same period of 11.87 percent.

Enough said. Let's just keep in mind that our eventual portfolio allocation will inevitably have some passive funds in it. But does that mean we are giving up on active management? Not a chance! What we are going to do instead is be smart and invest in actively managed funds where the market may be less efficient, that is, where the chance of finding a fund manager who beats her respective benchmark is greater than with the large companies that are more widely followed.

Bond Funds

We'll start with the relatively easy topic of bond funds. No matter who you are, or how long or short your investment time horizon is, it is likely that some part of your assets will be invested in bonds. Keep in mind that the philosophy here is not to achieve dazzling performance. Instead, what we are looking for is decent performance and little or no risk. The bond portion of your portfolio will act as ballast, as a safe harbor in the event of a storm, that part of your portfolio that will never be a source of unpleasant surprises.

Quality or High-Yield (Junk) Bonds?

Another important point: I am not going to recommend anything but quality bonds for your winning portfolio. There are plenty of bond funds, some high quality and some low quality—or as the low-quality variety are more commonly known, junk bonds. Junk bonds have higher yields (interest rates) than high-quality and U.S. government bonds because they are riskier. There is a greater chance that you won't get your money back when the bond matures if the company defaults on its loans or goes out of business. So to induce investors to buy these riskier bonds, the company just offers a higher interest rate.

One problem with junk bonds is that in recent years the spread—that is, the difference between the yields on high-quality bonds and the yield on junk bonds— has narrowed considerably so that the difference in the yield between the two extremes can be as little as 3 percent or even less. This happens because investors have become complacent about risk given that the economy has been growing for over six years and there have been few defaults on junk bonds. In my view—and that of many other investment professionals—the yield on junk bonds is not high enough to justify the risk you are assuming in owning them. In an economic down-turn, which we cannot predict with any accuracy, more companies will get into trouble and there will be more defaults on junk bonds issued by these troubled companies. A bond that stops paying interest becomes very close to worthless. Your only hope is that the company subsequently reorganizes or liquidates and there are enough assets to pay off the bondholders, even if it is only pennies on the dollar.

For our purposes, we want to confine the risk-taking to the equity (and, in some cases, the commodity) portion of the portfolio. We want very little risk in the bond portion.

Bond Maturity and Duration

A bond's maturity is simply the date on which the issuer of the bond has to pay your money back. (You will have received your interest payments twice a year in the meantime.) So, if you buy a 10-year bond in January 2008, you get your money back in January 2018. Real simple.

Now the longer the maturity of a bond, the greater is its sensitivity to interest rates. This makes sense. Suppose you buy a bond that has a coupon, or interest rate, of 5 percent. Why 5 percent? Because that's what the market says the interest should be to sell the bond today. Put another way, that's what investors expect to receive to induce them to buy your bond. That interest rate is based on the current market conditions.

But conditions change. Suppose you buy the bond and two years from now interest rates go up. New issuers of bonds will have to pay investors 6 percent because interest rates went up. What does that mean for your bond that pays only 5 percent? It means its value will go down. The market price of your bond, which came out at 100, will now be closer to 95 or 96, so that someone who buys it from you will get an effective yield closer to 6 percent, which is what the market pays currently. Of course, this example works the other way too. If interest rates go down, say to 4 percent, your bond with a 5 percent coupon will go up in value, to reflect the fact that new bonds are coming out at 4 percent.

Another example: a three-month Treasury bill isn't going to change in value because you'll get your money back in three months. If interest rates go up in the meantime, you can buy new T-bills when the ones you now own mature. By the way, that's called "rolling them over." Similarly, one- and two-year bonds don't vary much in price and value because their maturity dates are near. These are short-term bonds. Intermediate-term bonds are those with maturities of 5 to 10 years. Long-term bonds have maturities in excess of 10 years up to 30 years.

We will focus on short- to intermediate-term bonds to minimize the interest rate risk of long-term bonds.

Duration is a measure of interest rate risk. You only need to remember that a bond with a duration of 12 years means that if interest rates rise 1 percent, the value of your bond may decrease by 12 percent. If the duration is 10 years and the interest rates go up 1 percent, your bond might decline by 10 percent and so forth. This is a simpler way to judge your bond's sensitivity to interest rates than average yields that require a myriad of calculations to come up with the same statistic. So when considering a bond, or a bond fund, check the duration of the bond or the portfolio. In this case, a lower duration is safer than a higher one.

Bond Fund Choices

With bond funds, as with stock funds, we face the choice of active versus passive investing. With bonds, the choice is easier. Passive funds, those that mirror an index, are a safer choice since we are not looking for spectacular performance, but for safety and income. Choices here will include:

- Vanguard Intermediate Bond Index Fund
- Vanguard Short-Term Bond Index Fund

I cite these two simply as examples. There are other bond funds that will do just as well. However I am a bit gun-shy about recommending specific funds in a book, as opposed to a magazine or newspaper article. If I mention funds in this book, it is because they have a long track record and I am confident their performance will be the same now as when the book is available.

When we put together our winning portfolio for your particular goals, we will limit ourselves to high-quality short bond funds or intermediate bond funds in order to minimize the risk of interest rate changes and use this part of the portfolio as a safe harbor in the event of unusual stock market turbulence.

Equity Funds

The major part of your winning portfolio will be made up of equity securities, or funds that invest in stocks. We have learned that large-cap stocks are widely followed by Wall Street analysts. These stocks account for the major part of the stock market's performance as measured by an index like the S&P 500. The oldest major index, the Dow Jones Average, also measures the stock market's performance, but since that index only has 30 stocks, we tend to consider broader indexes as more representative of the movement of the market as a whole.

When I talked about market efficiency, I was talking about how hard it is to beat the stock market's performance by picking stocks and creating our own portfolio. The pros have a hard enough time doing it and few succeed over long periods of time. My conclusion is that it is tough to beat the market index because it consists of very large companies that are widely followed, so it is very difficult for anyone to get an information edge—that is, to learn something about a company that few others know. So for our winning portfolio, we are not going to try to beat the market, at least not when it comes to large-cap stocks. Instead, we will buy an index fund, like the Vanguard 500 Index Fund we discussed earlier in this chapter, to fill the slot for large-cap stocks.

Are we throwing in the towel? Are we conceding defeat in our effort to achieve superior stock market performance? No. We are making a tactical decision as to which battle we want to fight. We are going to concede the large-cap battle and win the war on another battlefield. We will look for superior performance in areas where we believe that talented active managers can deliver superior performance and beat their respective benchmarks. With the index funds, we'll save a good amount of fees in the process, and we can devote our time and energy to finding superior talent in areas where we are more likely to encounter success.

How To Pick a Mutual Fund

In this section, we will talk about picking equity/stock funds. This category includes all of the different styles and types of stock funds we are likely to include in the winning portfolio, plus selected commodities funds, now and in the future. Among the categories we will consider are:

- **Large-cap funds.** For this category we are going to use index funds.
- **Small-cap funds:** These funds consist of stocks of smaller companies subdivided by style
  - Small-cap growth
  - Small-cap value
  - Blends

- **Mid-cap funds:** These funds consist of stocks of medium-sized companies subdivided by style
  - Mid-cap growth
  - Mid-cap value
  - Blends
- **International funds:** These include funds that buy stocks in countries all over the world, but mostly in developed countries and markets
  - International growth
    - Small cap
    - Large cap
    - Blends
  - International value
    - Small cap
    - Large cap
    - Blends
- **Emerging markets funds:** These will be the riskiest funds in your portfolio and will accordingly have a smaller allocation than other categories.
- **Commodities funds:** We will recommend only gold and energy in this category.

So how do we pick the right funds in these categories? There are over 6,000 funds to choose from! So we have our work cut out for us, don't we? One way to approach this conundrum is to hire a professional investment advisor to help you through the choices. Again, we'll talk about the pros and cons of doing that in Chapter 9.

Getting It Right

There are some important criteria you need to know to pick the right mutual funds. This process is complicated by advice and natural inclinations that are not well suited to the task. For example, the first thing most people look for in picking a winning fund is the fund's most recent track record. Magazines, TV commentators, and Internet sites highlight the best-performing funds of the last year or two, and invariably money flows in to these heralded winners. Is that a good way to pick a fund? Definitely not. Often, a fund that tops the list of winners did so because it featured an industry that was in favor over the past year. For example, in recent years energy funds soared to the top of the performance list when oil prices tripled. Likewise gold. Now both of these industries are among those I believe should have an appropriate allocation in a winning portfolio, but many investors, after witnessing the most recent performance, proceeded to bet the ranch on these winners. The fact is that most of them do not repeat. Picking funds based on their most recent splendid performance is not a good way to pick a fund that is likely to be a future winner. Studies have shown that funds that performed well over a particular period had no more than a 50/50 chance of repeating their good performance in subsequent periods.

So when we seek out winning funds, it is important to know what to look for. Among the characteristics you need to focus on are:

- Good performance record over several years
- Good results compared to the fund's peers
- Consistency of management
- Low turnover of stocks in the portfolio
- Risk that is no greater and preferably lower than the stock market as a whole

Screening

So, how do you pick a mutual fund? Many investors, professionals included, pick funds and stocks by a process

SCREENING ONLINE

The screening process can be accomplished through several online sites. Among those that I like are Money.cnn.com, Kiplinger.com and Morningstar.com. Morningstar is devoted exclusively to mutual funds while Kiplinger's site has many other investment topics and some interesting and juicy articles on the entire spectrum of investing. (Please note: I know that Kiplinger's name is on the cover of this book but I have no affiliation with them and I recommend their site only because I like it.)

All three of these sites have mutual fund screens you can use. Screens can also be found at sites run by brokerage firms. I like the simplicity of the screening process at Schwab.com. As you might expect, the big fund families, like Vanguard, Fidelity, and T. Rowe Price, also have websites that allow you to select funds. The problem is that—big surprise—they only show the funds that they manage. You won't find a T. Rowe Price fund on the Fidelity website even if that happens to be the best one for your purposes. So stick with the sites that offer independent advice and whose screens cover all of the funds in a particular category based on the selections you make.

called *screening*. The best-known resource for mutual fund selection is Morningstar (www.Morningstar.com), which has both free and premium sites. Their mutual fund screen is powerful and available on the free part of the site. I will walk you through the choices on the Morningstar.com fund screen as I consider them useful and thorough.

First Criterion: Style You start by selecting criteria that are important to you in picking a fund to buy. First, of course, is style. Let's say we are shopping for a small-cap value fund. First, go to the Morningstar.com website. On the first page, click on the "Funds" tab at the top of the page. On the Funds page, look for the "Morningstar Tools" category. Under the "Morningstar Tools" heading, click on "Mutual Fund Screener." Once there, you will be at the "Set Criteria" tab. The first screen here will provide the following choices:

Fund group:
The choices range from domestic stock, international stock, taxable bonds, municipal bonds, balanced bonds, or all. Since we are shopping for a small-cap value fund, we start by picking "Domestic Stock."

Morningstar Category:
Different types of funds are listed. Choose: "Small Value."

Manager tenure greater than or equal to:
The choices range from "Any" and "Category average" to 1, 3, 5, and 10 years. Pick either Category average or 5 years. Shorter than five years isn't enough time to evaluate a manager. Few managers have managed the same fund for 10 years, so that isn't a useful choice. Category average is also an acceptable choice since it gives us the average tenure of this category of manager, or longer.

Second Criterion: Investment Minimums and Fund Expenses Most funds have some minimum investment requirements that you need to know to see if your contemplated purchase qualifies. Another important factor is the expense ratio of the fund you are contemplating. Remember that expenses detract from your fund's performance. Fund expenses may be inevitable, but lower is better.

Minimum initial purchase less than or equal to:
Choices range from $500 to $10,000. Pick one based on the size of your portfolio and the size of the investment

you will make in each of the funds you choose. If your personal minimum is high, pick $10,000 to eliminate institutional funds which often have extremely high minimums such as $1 million or more.

Load funds:

You are given the choice of considering both load funds and no-load funds, or no-loads exclusively. I don't have to tell you what the right answer is here, but I will anyway—No-load funds only!

Expense ratio less than or equal to:

The lower the expense ratio the better, but this screen isn't too helpful. We don't want to pick a fund primarily because its expense ratio is low. We are looking for talented managers, and while the expense ratio is important, it shouldn't be the driving force behind your decision to find a talented fund manager. The right choice here is "Category average" which means the average cost of this category or *lower.*

Third Criterion: RATING AND RISK Here the screen offers a choice among the Morningstar Star ratings, from ★ to ★★★★★.

Morningstar Star Rating:

Pick three, four, and five stars to ensure a choice among a wider variety of funds.

Fourth Criterion: Return These questions are of limited usefulness. You are going to be asked how much return you want from the funds. Well, DUH! Obviously, we want the highest return! But that's a dumb way to pick a fund since a high past return might not repeat in the future. Much better to find the steady-Eddies who

can be counted on to deliver good returns over long periods of time. So ignore the box that lets you put in a number, like 20 percent!

Here are the questions:

YTD return greater than or equal to:

You can write in your own number (but don't) or choose from:

- Any
- Category average
- S&P 500

"Any" is the best choice. Category average is generally acceptable, but remember, in this question you are being asked about year-to-date performance. Suppose we are in April. Year to date is pretty meaningless. In fact, a single year is not very meaningful. So this question is pointless. Choose "Any."

One-year return greater than or equal to:

Same choice as above. Same answer too. Pick "Any."

Three-year return greater than or equal to:

Now it gets more interesting. Here, the correct choice is "Category average" since over a three-year period or longer, you would hope that your fund is doing at least as well as the average fund in its category. Of course, if it is doing better, which we expect, then it will also show up on your screen based on this choice. The choice of "better than the S&P 500" is meaningless, since you are screening for a small-cap value fund and that style is different from the S&P 500 as is its performance, so a comparison between these "apples and oranges" indexes wouldn't tell us anything useful.

5-year return greater than or equal to:
Same answer as for three years only the five-year record is more meaningful.

10-year return greater than or equal to:
Again, same answer as for five years. Note however that your fund may not fall into this category because there are not many funds that have 10-year track records.

Fifth Criterion: Portfolio Funds have different "personalities" based on how much the manager buys and sells in a given year, how large the fund is in terms of assets under management, what types of stocks the fund buys—all part of what constitutes the fund's portfolio. You need to make some choices here as well.

Turnover less than or equal to:
Here the choices range from 25 percent to 150 percent plus selection of "Any" and "Category average." As you might assume, lower turnover is better than higher turnover since high turnover leads to higher taxes and greater costs for commissions on the transactions. But that doesn't mean that you should pick a turnover level. At the end of the day, the fund manager has to deliver a superior return to attract our attention. We shouldn't put ourselves in a position to tell the manager how much turnover he or she needs to achieve that result. Therefore, the right answer here is "Any."

Total assets less than or equal to:
With this question, you are being asked about the size of the fund you will consider investing in. The idea here is that a fund that is too small, say $100 million or less, may not be earning enough money to attract the best talent. A very large fund, say $5 billion or more, may

not have the flexibility to invest in smaller companies with great promise because the size of the fund would require it to make a very large dollar investment to make that purchase a meaningful position.

The choices offered range from $200 million to $5 billion. Over $5 billion for a small-cap fund is likely too large, so pick $5 billion or less.

Average market cap ($millions):
The question here is what size company can the fund buy? Size in this case is the total market capitalization of the company, or the value of all of the shares of the company multiplied by the share price. That tells you how much the company is worth in the marketplace. It also tells you how "liquid" the shares might be since companies with a higher value and a larger number of shares are likely to have more liquid and active markets than smaller companies.

The choices, however, aren't very useful. They range from market caps of $250 million and under to $10 billion or over. The problem is that there is no choice between $1 billion and $10 billion. We learned in Chapter 1 that the generally accepted opinion on small caps is that they include companies whose market capitalization is $3 billion or less. Since we are looking for a small-cap value fund, these choices are useless, so pick "Any." The fund manager will know what a small-cap market capitalization ought to be, so we can safely leave that choice to the manager.

Now What Happens?

We finished the choices, we made our selections, and we pushed the buttons, so what do we get? Those nice folks at Morningstar give us a list of funds that meet the criteria we plugged in. There are seven funds that passed our screens. But of the seven, only three are open to new investments. The others are closed to new investors because they have attracted as much money as they feel they can reasonably manage without hurting their fine records.

The three available choices are:

1. Columbia Small Cap Value
2. Gabelli Small Cap
3. Tamarack Micro Cap Value

The last fund, Tamarack, is a micro-cap fund which means it invests not in small companies, but tiny ones. We do not want to consider that category since it is highly risky and not in the category of small cap that we are seeking. That leaves us with two choices.

Please keep in mind that I am not recommending these specific funds because the choices you eventually make will be a function of what is good, appropriate, and available at the time you begin your own fund selection process. I am writing this in mid-2007 and I don't know when you will be reading it. As a result, I want to be sure you know the *process* for building your winning portfolio. If you do, choosing the rights funds will be a snap.

Commodity Funds

You will recall that I mentioned we would focus on only two commodities: energy and gold. There are several available funds in each of these categories. I like the Vanguard Energy Fund, even though it is quite large, because the team managing the fund is excellent and the fund has a fine record. This fund is actively managed. Also, for a fund of this type, the expense ratio is quite reasonable at less than 0.50 percent.

There are a number of gold funds available, including the Tocqueville Gold Fund, which also has a fine record.

Summing Up

Remember that we have not yet discussed the allocations for your fund, that is, how much of each type of fund you should use in your personal winning portfolio. That will depend on a number of factors, including your tolerance for risk and volatility and when you will need the money you are investing.

Another point: As I mentioned earlier, a number of different screening programs exist that you can use to pick funds. I chose the Morningstar screen as an example because, although I don't consider it perfect, it is well known and comprehensive and should help narrow down your choices if you input the data wisely. Feel free to try other screens and judge which ones suit you best.

In the next chapter, we will begin the process of putting together the elements of *your* winning portfolio. So get your hardhat and gloves, and let's start building!

Building Your Personal Winning Portfolio

Chapter 6

You won't be surprised to hear that a single portfolio will not be appropriate for everyone. So the task at hand is to build your personal portfolio, the one that will do what you want it to do in a time frame that fits your goals and dreams. In order to accomplish that mission, you and I will need to go through a process designed to identify your goals and to create the appropriate risk and time parameters for building your personal winning portfolio.

Let's start with one of the most important parameters: your time frame. Everyone who invests does so for a purpose. So the first thing we need to identify is what the money is for and how much time you need to get there. The possibilities are infinite. You might be saving for the college educations of your children, planning your retirement income, perhaps buying a vacation home, or yacht—or like a good friend of mine, amassing the funds to build and maintain an orphanage in India. The plan for whatever it is you are saving for will have a time when those funds are needed. That's your time frame. The plan will also have an assumed rate of return based on how much money you start with, how much you add along the way, and the amount of money

The first thing we need to identify is what the money is for and how much time you need to get there.

you expect at the end to fund your goal. That can be reduced to an expected rate of return.

Let's start with time frames. We'll talk in terms of ranges of time: short, intermediate, and long.

Short Term

We define short-term investment goals as those from one through three years. Assume that you have a short-term goal to buy an expensive car or perhaps you got a late start in funding your child's college education, and it's coming up soon.

You have seen from our earlier discussions that there is always some level of risk in investing in the stock market, whether you do it by buying stocks yourself or through a mutual fund or a money manager. Since no one can predict short-term market movements, we rely on time to bail us out—and it usually does. We know, for example, that over the past eighty years, stocks have risen about 10 percent a year. However, there were plenty of years when there was no gain at all and there were even years that included losses. You might remember that stocks went down three years in a row in 2000, 2001, and 2002.

So here's the bad news—one to three years just isn't enough time to take the risk that most portfolios will entail. It just isn't wise for you to risk your money in stocks if you only have one or two years to invest.

Most competent investment advisors will invariably suggest that for short periods, you avoid market risk. In this case, a portfolio will consist mostly of risk-free U.S. government bills and notes, mostly with short maturities or bank CDs. Of course, nothing stops you from speculating on good stock market performance for short periods of time. But doing so is just that—speculation.

Probably not an appropriate use of your hard-earned funds. So for short periods of time, stick to risk-free or very-low-risk securities, which will be primarily fixed-income securities.

Intermediate Term

We define intermediate-term investment goals as those between 4 through 10 years. Let's assume that you need between 5 and 10 years to achieve your goal. This is a time frame we can work with. In this portfolio, we will favor those asset classes whose standard deviations are on the low side. (Refer back to page 28 if you need a refresher on standard deviations.) We will have a portfolio that will hold stocks, likely through both passive and active mutual funds. Doing so will help us minimize the chances of poor or negative returns over our chosen time frame. This portfolio will assume some risk, since there is enough time for problems to work out. But it is likely to be somewhat less risky than the longer-term portfolios, which allow more time for markets to return to their normal earnings patterns.

Long Term

We define long-term investment goals as those that require between 10 and 30 years or longer to achieve. Long-term investing is the real sweet spot of the investment process. The reason is that if you select and allocate your portfolio wisely, it is hard to go wrong when time is on your side. The trick is getting it right and staying on top of the allocation as years go by.

A long-term portfolio vastly increases your chances of achieving your goal. In this type of portfolio we can employ a variety of asset classes, from very low risk to

One to three years just isn't enough time to take the risk that most portfolios will entail.

A long-term portfolio vastly increases your chances of achieving your goal.

> ### WHAT ABOUT TAXES?
>
> It is beyond the scope of this book to give tax advice, but that doesn't mean we should ignore taxes. They are a sad reality of investment life. It goes without saying that you should shelter as much of your investment income as you legally can. This will be accomplished though Simple IRAs, Roth IRAs, 401(k)s, and other pension vehicles. Take advantage of every opportunity to defer taxes on your investments. We have not assumed taxes in your earnings projections in this book.

risky, knowing that the combination of asset classes and their noncorrelating features will help move this portfolio toward achieving your winning goal. As you can tell, I truly hope that your investment goals are long term. That's the most likely way to amass a fortune, especially if you add to your portfolio over time.

Time To Talk about Risk (Again)

We have seen that we characterize risk in investments by historic standard deviation, or volatility. We do that because as hard as we try or pretend that we can, we can't really predict the future. So when analyzing the risk in any given type of investment, we look at the past. How has this asset class—say, large-cap stocks—performed over time? We look at the highs and lows and we come up with a volatility measure. The idea is that asset classes with low historic volatility will likely continue to have low volatility because that's how they are and that's how they behave, and vice versa. We conclude, therefore, that there is lower risk in the asset class with relatively low volatility than there is with those with higher volatility.

So we can reduce risk by picking asset classes and managers or funds whose historic volatility is low and whose performance is not highly correlated to one another. We can combine these low-volatility candidates with some others that may come with higher risk but where the returns are higher too. As always, it is the asset allocation that will drive the results, not only the returns but also the risk level of the portfolio as a whole.

That's about it for the investment theory stuff. Now we get into the realm of psychology. If I sound like I am prying into your subconscious it isn't because I want to be the investment version of Dr. Phil. The fact is that our reaction to risk is an emotion and each of us, as individuals, reacts in our own way. I am willing to bet that no matter what your level of investment experience, you have heard the expression "risk tolerance." It is an expression bandied about by all sorts of investment advisors to characterize pretty much what it says: your tolerance for risk. In this case, however, we are dealing with emotions. Can you tolerate a riskier portfolio or not? Now in classic investment theory, greater risk is necessary to achieve a greater return, but if you are going to be petrified by the higher volatility of the riskier portfolio, is it really worth it?

There are a number of questionnaires that address this subject and most investment advisors have access to one they like. It will ask questions such as: How awful would you feel if your portfolio went down 10 percent in any given year? Would that be acceptable to you? A few years go I wrote a book on behavioral investing entitled *The Wealth Equation*. I teamed up with

The fact is that our reaction to risk is an emotion and each of us, as individuals, reacts in our own way.

RISK TOLERANCE QUIZZES YOU CAN ACCESS ONLINE

There are a number of websites that offer risk tolerance quizzes. The majority requires that you give personal information that could lead to spam emails or junk mail, or they require a subscription to the site, which isn't worth doing if it's just to take one quiz.

Here are some free websites that do not require registration. Since these tests are free, you may find it useful to take a few of them. My colleague, Deborah Pierdominici, did the research on these sites and here are her insights:

■ *http://www.efgi.com/personal/investing/ questionnaire.html:* This test is easy to follow and offers instant results with tidy explanations.

■ *http://www.partnervest.com/Risk-Tolerance-Questionnaire.html:* This test is not for an investment novice. Most questions have a direct-investment focus; it doesn't ask many questions regarding the more emotional side of investing. In addition, the questions and result explanations use many undefined financial/investment terms.

■ *http://moneycentral.msn.com/investor/ calcs/n_riskq/main.asp:* This test on the MSN Money website is practical and helpful. It asks a lot of questions similar to those on other questionnaires.

■ *http://www.webcalcs.com/cgi-bin/calcs/ prod/risk.cgi?client=safecoplaza:* This is a website for Torrid Technologies, which appears to make various types of calculation software. The test is free and didn't require registration or personal information. Some questions seem rather silly. If you are put off by this, just remember that they are probably designed to gauge emotional response and level of caution. Also, the results came with very short explanations.

The site myrisktolerance.com charges a small fee (currently $16) and the test might be worth it. It is quite comprehensive and asks 25 questions of varying complexity. What you get at the end is a bell curve showing where you rank in risk tolerance on a scale of 1 to 100. I suggest you try the free tests and gauge how happy you are with the results before spending money on this one.

a noted financial behavior expert, Shoya Zichy, who created some tests that are a derivative of the Myers Briggs personality profiles.

If you aren't sure of your risk tolerance, it might be a good idea to take one of these tests. Most brokerage and investment firms have a version of a risk tolerance test that also includes questions about your investment time frame and other important information that will be part of your decision on how to invest. In my experience, many individuals are very tolerant of risk when the market is going up! Their tolerance seems to fade dramatically when the market reverses trend.

It is very important to know yourself when it comes to risk. One of the reasons this is so important is that if you pick an otherwise fine long-term portfolio that is too risky for your personal psyche, there is the danger that you will sell out all of your holdings in a mild panic when a major market correction comes along. I should add that when individuals do that, they either never get back into the market or they do so when the market has behaved well for such a long period of time that they are likely to get back in at the top. Incidentally, have you ever wondered why everybody doesn't get rich in the stock market? The simple fact is that most investors don't have the nerve to stick it out. They either listen to bad advice, fancy themselves stock market timing experts, or panic out at the first sign of a weak market. So again, it is important to know who you are and how you will react to the inevitable declines along the way.

The way to build a portfolio with an eye on risk is to prepare different portfolios according to their risk profile. For our purposes, we will use three models—conservative, moderate, and aggressive. The titles tell the story. The portfolios will be designed and built based on two factors:

1. Time horizon
2. Risk tolerance

WHAT'S WITH THOSE GREEK LETTERS?

You may have heard conversations about the stock market and stocks in general that include terms like *alpha* and *beta*. Of the two terms, beta is the better known and most frequently used. Alpha has become popular more recently.

Beta measures a stock's or portfolio's volatility compared to the stock market as a whole. You can use any well-known stock market index to measure beta, and the most popular one is the S&P 500. So if the benchmark, say the S&P 500, has a value of 1.0, a beta of 1.2 means that your stock, or your portfolio, is 20 percent more volatile than the stock market. A beta of 0.80 means that your stock's volatility is less than the volatility of the stock market. Remember that one important way we measure risk is volatility, so a stock with a lower volatility than the stock market's suggests that the stock is less risky than the market as a whole.

Alpha is a measure of performance. If we have a fund or money manager who is producing excellent results, we really want to know how much of those results is due to the stock market as a whole and how much is due to the brilliance of our manager. Now if we ask the manager that question, I'm pretty sure I know what he'll say. So I need another source. Alpha measures the return we got that is *not* attributable to the stock market's performance. Alpha tells us how much added value the manager gave us over and above what the market did. Thus, an alpha higher than 0 tells us that the manager has added value. An alpha below 0 tells us that he subtracted value.

The shorter the time horizon, the more conservative the portfolio should be. And the lower the risk tolerance, the more conservative the portfolio should be. An individual who has a long-term horizon and a moderate amount of risk tolerance will likely want a moderate portfolio. An investor who can genuinely tolerate ups and downs in the market and has a longer-term investment objective may well opt for the aggressive portfolios.

Remember that in modern portfolio theory, you only get rewarded for taking risk but there is no guarantee that this will happen. So we assume that if we build the portfolio properly, the more aggressive portfolio will have a higher return than the moderate portfolio, which in turn will have a higher return than the conservative portfolio.

The first part of our building process, the first building block if you will, is going to be risk, which in turn will be influenced by our investment time horizon. Once we have a handle on that part of the objective, we can begin populating the portfolio with appropriate asset classes in the appropriate amounts.

Monte Carlo Simulation

There is a major, relatively new tool used in portfolio construction with an unfortunate name for an investment process: Monte Carlo simulation. I call it unfortunate since using an investment tool named after a famous casino might not inspire confidence, but let's put that thought aside. This tool is a remarkable step forward in assessing risk and the probability of achieving a desired investment result.

Let's take the long-term record for the stock market performance of about 10 percent a year. We'll use this for planning purposes. One of the biggest problems in financial planning and portfolio construction is that even if we are absolutely right about this projected return, we know it will not occur in a straight line. That is, stocks are not going to go up a steady 10 percent each and every year. We are simply saying that the average return will be 10 percent. Now here's the problem: The *timing* of the ups and down can have a major impact on the overall performance even if we are absolutely right about the average return of 10 percent.

Let me share with you an example I used in my book *Investment Gurus:* I am going to offer you a choice of investment managers. Manager A has had average annual returns over the past five years of 14 percent. We have every confidence that his record will continue this way over the next five years, so take this as an assumption in this exercise. Manager B has had an average annual return of 9 percent over the past five years and, here again, we expect that her record will continue over the next five years, so let's assume that to be the case. Your challenge is to determine which of these managers you would pick based on their past performance?

Dumb question, right? Maybe not. Let's have a look at the five-year record of each of these managers. Manager A is the guy with the 14 percent average annual performance over the past five years and here's his record year by year:

Manager A

Year	Performance
1	20%
2	40%
3	20%
4	−50%
5	40%

Our first observation is that this is a very volatile manager. His performance was terrific until year 4 when he lost a whopping 50 percent. Fortunately, he recovered somewhat the following year, year 5, with a gain of 40 percent.

So how did he do? Let's recalculate his average annual return. Just add up the year-to-year performance and divide by 5. His return was 14 percent a year.

Now let's look at Manager B, the one with the 9 percent average return. Here's her record:

| | Manager B |
Year	Performance
1	9%
2	9%
3	9%
4	9%
5	9%

Talk about consistency! This manager delivers a 9 percent return with clockwork precision. Her average performance over 5 years doesn't require a calculator—it's 9 percent.

The question that interests us most, of course, is which manager made the most money. If you guessed it was the guy with the average performance of 14 percent, you guessed wrong. Let me demonstrate. The best way to see who made the most money is to use a geometric progression, one which will show us dollars, not percentages. The easiest way to do this is to start out with a baseline of 100 for each manager, apply the appropriate percentages, and see what happens. Assume the base 100 is $100.

Year	Manager A	Base 100	Manager B	Base 100
1	20%	120	9%	109
2	40%	168	9%	119
3	20%	202	9%	129.5
4	–50%	101	9%	141
5	40%	141	9%	154

Surprise! Manager B, the one with the 9 percent annual return, made more money than Manager A, who had average annual returns of 14 percent. So the first point to remember is that when somebody talks about

You can't rely on average returns, even over a long period of time, to be confident about your future returns.

"average annual returns," look for another method of calculating the results.

I took you through the return exercise to make an important point. You can't rely on average returns, even over a long period of time, to be confident about your future returns. I have often mentioned that stocks have a long-term record of more than 10 percent a year, and I am confident that stocks will continue to do very well in the future. But since the stock market could be up 30 percent or down 30 percent in any given year, the *timing* of these events will greatly influence your returns.

Think about it. If you started investing in the early 1990s, you would have spectacular 10-year results even if you only invested in an index fund. That's because the '90s was the best decade in stock market history with performance of around 18 percent a year. But what if you had started investing in 2000 instead? Your investment program would have started with three consecutive years of decline and your portfolio would likely have gone down by 40 percent or more, simply based on the overall stock market performance during that period. A 40 percent decline is hard to make up. Remember that a 50 percent decline requires a 100 percent gain just to get back even. So when we say that your stocks may well earn an average of 8 percent or 10 percent in coming years, that's all well and good, and it may well happen, but we can be pretty sure that it won't happen in a straight, linear fashion like Manager B's 9 percent each year.

What Monte Carlo simulations do is compute the many different variables in a given portfolio, including the ones we have just talked about. What if we encounter serious declines early on? What if we have five years of bad returns in a row? What if we have five years of terrific returns in a row? How can I get a handle on how all these different variables might affect my personal portfolio performance? The Monte Carlo simulation calculates thousand and thousands of permutations of each of your asset classes, using either historical assumptions or the ones we put in, and figures out not the average expected return of your portfolio, but a *range* of returns for thousands of different permutations a portfolio might take, given all of the different possibilities that may occur over the years you are invested.

The chart on the following page is an example of three portfolios on which we have done a Monte Carlo simulation. The three portfolios are conservative, moderate, and aggressive.

The allocations I use in this example are basic stock/bond/commodity allocations that I will use for illustrative purposes. Later on, I will refine these allocations to create your personal portfolio.

You will notice three pie charts at the bottom of the chart. The investment industry could not survive without pie charts. The table right above the pie charts shows the allocation of each of the three portfolios— conservative, moderate, and aggressive. As you might expect, the conservative portfolio is heavily weighted toward bonds while the aggressive portfolio is heavily weighted toward stocks.

Right under the allocation table is a table entitled Performance. That tells us that we expect the conservative portfolio to earn an average of 6.4 percent a year, the moderate portfolio to earn 8.7 percent, and the aggressive portfolio 10.9 percent on average each year. The last line shows the estimated standard deviation for the different portfolios. Here again, the conservative portfolio has a lower standard deviation than the higher ones, meaning that the conservative portfolio is less risky that the more aggressive portfolios. (A lower standard

Portfolio Allocations

	Conservative	Moderate	Aggressive
Stocks	20.00	50.00	45.00
International Equity	0.00	10.00	30.00
Domestic Fixed Income	80.00	40.00	10.00
Energy/Gold	0.00	0.00	15.00

Performance

	Conservative	Moderate	Aggressive
Return	6.40	8.70	10.90
Std. Dev.	5.57	9.60	11.95

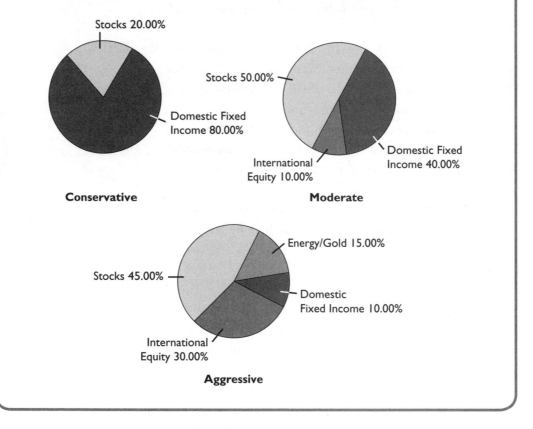

deviation signals a less risky portfolio than does a higher standard deviation.) And hopefully without beating this point to death, remember that you get rewarded for risk, so the riskier portfolio ought to provide a higher return than the less risky one.

Now we say that the average return for the conservative portfolio is 6.4 percent, but we know that it won't produce that return each and every year. So what might it return in any given year? That's where the Monte Carlo simulations come in. It does thousands of calculations and permutations to come up with all of the likely probabilities of what these portfolios might return in all kinds of different market environments. We attribute the likelihood that returns will fall within these ranges at 90 percent, which means that in catastrophic or euphoric scenarios, there is a 5 percent chance it could be better than the best extreme and 5 percent chance it could be worse than the worst case. Put another way, there is a 95 percent chance that your portfolio will do *better* than the worst case in the range.

Now look at the chart on the following page. This chart again shows conservative, moderate, and aggressive portfolios but in this case with a bunch of ragged lines. There are actually thousands of these lines in each chart but you can't see them all because so many of them overlap along the way. What the simulation has done is chart the course for all of the different permutations this simple portfolio might take over the next 20 years given what we know about the historic behavior of the included asset classes. The only problem is that we don't know which of the possible paths this portfolio will take because we can't predict the future! Yet you can appreciate how valuable this tool is because it gives us, with a confidence factor of 90 percent, the range of outcomes for any similarly configured portfolio. The dark line in the middle of each of the three charts is the middle line, or the most likely course.

Annualized Simulated Performance Over 20 Years

	Conservative			Moderate			Aggressive		
	5th Percentile	50th Percentile	95th Percentile	5th Percentile	50th Percentile	95th Percentile	5th Percentile	50th Percentile	95th Percentile
1 Year	−2.00	6.24	15.81	−5.71	7.95	25.13	−6.44	10.44	31.87
5 Year	2.25	6.27	10.55	1.57	8.34	15.53	1.53	10.37	19.75
10 Year	3.35	6.10	9.10	3.58	8.15	13.01	4.05	10.22	16.26
15 Year	3.93	6.07	8.52	4.19	8.06	12.08	5.07	10.09	15.27
20 Year	4.23	6.18	8.26	4.85	8.20	11.60	5.92	10.23	14.67

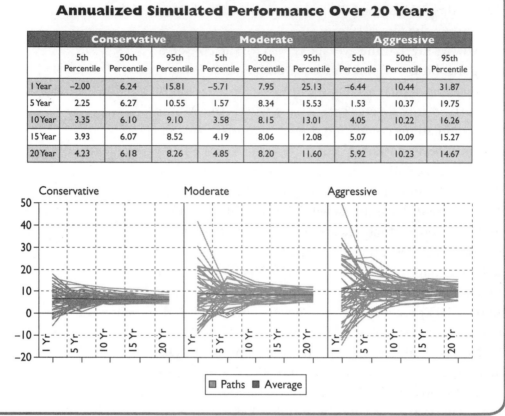

So what is the message to take away from this? Look at the middle line in each portfolio and at the box at the top of the chart to see the expected return over 20 years for each of the three portfolios. The annualized returns (over 20 years) are about 6 percent for the conservative portfolio, 8 percent for the moderate one, and 10 percent for the aggressive portfolio. Now look at the extremes. Don't pay too much attention to the highest line; that one tells us what we might earn over 20 years if everything goes our way. That would be the case if each of these asset classes does as well as it might ever do during the entire 20-year period. I know you'll just love that outcome, so let's not spend a lot of time on it. Look instead at the lowest line. That would be the 5th percentile number at the bottom of the box. This is our near worst-case scenario. This is what might happen if everything went as bad as it could get for the full 20 years. In that sorry case, the conservative portfolio would return almost 2 percent a year for 20 years, the moderate portfolio would return nothing, but you wouldn't lose any money either, and the aggressive portfolio would earn a fraction of 1 percent each year. Granted, there is a 95 percent chance you will do better than the worst case in this simulation, but if you like to know what the worst case might be, there you have it.

Incidentally, some of the lines in the simulation are "off the chart," so to speak. These represent the 0 percent and 100 percent possibilities that are very remote and unlikely. As a result, we use the 5 percent to 95 percent probabilities in most of the simulations.

The foregoing exercise introduced you to Monte Carlo simulations. These statistical devices are very helpful in analyzing likely future returns. It can help increase both your knowledge and your confidence in the investment process. I will show you examples of Monte Carlo simulation in your personal portfolios but in a different form in the next chapter. Now it's time to move to your own personal winning portfolio.

Your Personal Winning Portfolio

You've learned the basics, you know about risk, you've been brainwashed about the importance of diversification. Now the time has come to build your personal portfolio. First, I need to assume an initial amount to be invested. For the smaller initial portfolio we will have fewer asset classes and the model will be somewhat simpler than for the larger portfolio where we can diversify with a greater number of different investments. In the smaller portfolio we won't diversify by style as much as we might with the larger portfolios. For example, in the small portfolio, we can pick a diversified mutual fund which will include both large and small cap, and value and growth styles, and not be concerned about having separate funds for each style or class.

I am going to assume three starting levels of investment. Of course, I can't know *exactly* how much money you will start your investment program with, so pick the amount that is closest to your circumstances. To cover a broad range of possibilities, I have chosen the following starting points:

1. $7,000
2. $60,000
3. $250,000

Once you pick one of them, you can then "tweak" it according to any personal preferences you might have, but don't go overboard. These portfolios are carefully designed to do what you want them to do. I also assume that you will continue to save and add to your portfolio regularly, possibly every month. So I will also provide an amount of money you will save and add to your portfolio each month. These amounts will be detailed in the next chapter.

Of all the different asset classes that are appropriate for your portfolio, we need to decide how much of each selected asset class your portfolio will require. Once again, here is the list of choices from Chapter 5:

- **Large-cap funds**
  - Vanguard 500 Index Fund
- **Small-cap funds**
  - Small-cap growth
  - Small-cap value
  - Blends
- **Mid-cap funds**
  - Mid-cap growth
  - Mid-cap value
  - Blends
- International funds
  - International growth
    - Small cap
    - Large cap
    - Blends
  - International value
    - Small cap
    - Large cap
    - Blends
- **Emerging markets funds**
- **Commodities funds**
  - Vanguard Energy Fund
  - Gold fund
- **Stocks you choose on your own**

You will recall that the two most important factors in choosing the right portfolio will be time and risk tolerance. Based on all of our earlier discussions, how would you characterize your risk tolerance? Not sure? Let's see if I can help. If we start with your time frame for the money, I can guide you to the right risk level and we'll deal with the emotional side of this decision a little later. Are you investing for five years or so? Choose conservative. Is your time frame around

Most investors don't get rich because they abandon their investment program somewhere along the way.

10 years? This could be the time frame for your child's college education or money to start a business, or funds for a second home. With this in mind, choose moderate as your risk level. Are you investing for longer than 10 years? This would be the case if you are investing for your eventual retirement or if you are starting this process at a very young age, and if so, let me not miss this opportunity to compliment you on your wisdom. Indeed, if you are among the younger readers of this book and you follow your investment program religiously, I am certain of one thing: You will become not well off, but rich. If you are investing for more than 10 years, choose either moderate (for now) or aggressive.

Why the choice of moderate or aggressive? Because we are now dealing with emotional factors. Earlier, I mentioned to you that a fair question for any skeptical investor to ask is this: With all of the investment books out there, and with all of the advice emanating from investment guys and gals in fancy suits and posh offices, how come everybody doesn't get rich in the stock market? A fair question indeed. My answer is simply that most investors don't get rich because even if they find a good investment program (which I can immodestly say that you have done), they simply do not stick to it.

To phrase the question another way, will you get rich reading this book? The answer is YES. You just have to do one thing: Follow the advice and, most important, STICK TO IT! Most investors don't get rich because they abandon their investment program somewhere along the way. More often than not, they abandon their investment goal because of fear. Just as sure as the sun will rise tomorrow, the stock market will go through some really bad times and many investors will get out "while they can." The only difference between stock market declines and the sun rising tomorrow is that we know exactly what time the sun will rise tomorrow, and we haven't got a clue when the stock market is going to embark on one of its periodic swan dives.

Do not stray and do not panic when everything seems to be coming apart. Remember history. You may not be old enough to remember the Kennedy assassination, the 1973–1974 major market decline, or the 1987 stock market crash. Even if you aren't old enough to remember any of them, you are old enough to remember September 11, 2001, and the tremendous market decline and trauma that followed that tragic event. We survived all of those disasters and the wealthy winners are those who stayed invested. So forgive me if I beat the drum endlessly on this point, but I owe it to you and it is important to me that you heed this point above all.

Back to the psychology of the moment. If your investment objective is long term—10 years or longer—and if you believe you have the ability to withstand a major market meltdown and continue with your investment program, than you should pick the aggressive portfolio. Go back to page 102 and look at the Monte Carlo simulation with the ragged lines. Look at the different permutations again and at the numbers in the box at the bottom with the returns and time frames. Assuming this is your portfolio, if you think you can live through the worst case scenarios and not lose too much sleep, then choose the more aggressive portfolio.

The next subject to think about is whether or not you want to select stocks for your portfolio yourself. You already know my preference: I believe in leaving the stock picking to professionals who spend all day thinking about it. Yet I recognize that some individuals want to spend the time picking stocks they like, and they just might be good at it. Are you one of them? Perhaps you have an expertise in a particular area where you would be in a good position to recognize a new discovery or a transformative corporate development a company might have made. If you are in this category, take about 10 percent of the equity allocation in the portfolio you select and manage it yourself.

Summing Up

So far we have discussed three criteria for your portfolio: risk tolerance, time horizon, and whether or not you want to pick stocks yourself. In the next chapter, you will find a detailed roadmap to select the personal portfolio that is right for you. You will see all of the following:

■ Your personal winning portfolio allocation by asset class
■ A projection of the future returns and risk of your portfolio

We discussed the possibility that some of you will want to buy stocks on your own. If you are among them, just take 10 percent of the portfolio we allocated to stocks and use that for your own stock picks. We will assume in our projections that your selections will do as well as the stocks managed by the professional investors. So good luck!

Note also that I am including not one, but two 20 and 30 year projections for the larger long term portfolios. That way, you can look up how much your portfolio is likely to be worth as the years go by. This should provide a good incentive for you to continue. Why *two* projections?

The first projection is based mostly on the historical returns of the asset classes you will be invested in. You know by now that these returns may vary widely from year to year, so the accuracy of these predictions is much higher for the longer time frames. But that first projection assumes simple asset class returns, in other words, whatever the market has done in the past. It does not include any "value added," or incremental earnings, due to manager talent. Recall that we are going to use index funds for the large-cap portion (value and growth) of your portfolio because it is so hard to beat the market, as measured by the Standard and Poor 500 Index. So we're not going to try, since by doing so we stand a greater chance of having a *worse* performance than the market as a whole. For the other asset classes in your portfolio, I am going to assume that you will choose mutual funds with talented managers who will earn their keep, and their fees, by beating their respective benchmarks. By how much will they beat their benchmark? Who knows? To be safe, we will assume they only beat it by 2 percent on average a year. Not too much to ask, right?

So turn the page, read the brief instructions, find your personal winning portfolio, and start investing!

Putting Your Personal Winning Portfolio Together

n the following pages you will select your personal portfolio. Here's how to choose:

I am assuming three starting levels for your investment program:

1. $7,000
2. $60,000
3. $250,000

I realize that your personal starting point is not likely to be exactly one of these amounts, so pick the one that comes closest to the amount of money you will start with. I have also assumed that you will add to this amount on a monthly basis as follows:

■ **$7,000 Portfolio**
- – $200 a month in the first five years
- – $300 a month in years 5–10
- – $400 a month in years 10–15
- – $500 a month in years 15–30

- **$60,000 Portfolio**
  - $250 a month in the first 5 years
  - $500 a month in years 5–10
  - $1,000 a month in years 10–15
  - $1,500 a month in years 15–30

- **$250,000 Portfolio**
  - $500 a month in the first 5 years
  - $1,000 a month in years 5–10
  - $1,500 a month in years 10–15
  - $3,000 a month in years 15–30

Now pick your time frame. Remember that we are not going to create a portfolio for short-term time objectives since, in the short term, markets are so unpredictable that any degree of market risk is not advisable. So here are the choices:

- Intermediate term: 5 to 10 years
- Long term: 10 years and longer

Next, pick your level of risk tolerance:

- Conservative
- Moderate
- Aggressive

As we discussed, if you want to buy some stocks on your own, just take 10 percent of the portfolio we allocated to stocks and use that for your own stock picks. We will assume in our projections that your selections will do as well as the stocks managed by the professional investors.

The index on page 114 will tell you where you will find information on your chosen investment program.

A WORD ABOUT INFLATION

I have not presented "inflation-adjusted" returns in this chapter and many of you astute readers will notice that. Inflation-adjusted returns would provide dollar amounts that have been reduced by the inflation effect in the future. In other words, if $1,000 won't buy as much in 10 or 20 years as it does today, what would the purchasing power of that $1,000 be in the future? The reason I didn't add that calculation is that I felt it would add yet another set of analyses to an already crowded chapter. I don't want to confuse you; I just want you to get rich by building your winning portfolio. So for those who would have liked an extra set of inflation-adjusted tables, I apologize. Just remember that even with mild inflation, the dollars I expect you to earn over time will be worth somewhat less in the future.

For example, if you chose $60,000 as your initial investment, go to page 135 for information on issues particular to this investment level. Then, if you decided on an aggressive risk tolerance with long-term goals, you'll find the discussion of the asset allocation and the projection of future returns on page 141.

INDEX

Starting Level 1:
Initial Investment of $7,000

Since this portfolio starts with the relatively small amount of $7,000, we can't realistically use mutual funds for the allocations because the amounts will be too small to meet the minimums of most mutual funds. So we will use exchange-traded funds (ETFs) instead. (See Chapter 1, page 18 for a refresher on what these are.) These can be bought the same way stocks are bought, through a broker, preferably online because the commission cost will be lower.

As for returns, in most cases these return assumptions are based on the history of returns for each of the respective asset classes. In some cases, the historic return has been adjusted to represent the way the current environment has changed. A good example is fixed income and inflation. The historic return for bonds is quite high since it takes into account the very high bond returns of the 1970s and early 1980s when inflation was rampant. I don't think it is prudent to assume that that high level of inflation will return any time soon, therefore I have used a lower number for the future expected return of bonds as well as for inflation.

Standard deviation measures the risk and volatility of the particular asset class. Historic volatility values are also being used here. Remember, the higher the number, the more volatile and riskier the asset class is.

In the chart with the Monte Carlo simulation, you will see the expected return, as well as the range of returns for the portfolio over different time periods. Take a look at what the worst-case scenario, percent-loss would be in any given year (the 5th percentile) and make sure this is in line with your risk tolerance. But always keep in mind that statistically, your portfolio has a 95 percent chance to do *better* than this worst-case scenario, and only a 5 percent chance it could do worse. Also note that as time goes by, the range gap closes *dramatically*. Remember, time is your friend! These statistics should make it easier for you to make an investment decision you can live with.

The table below shows examples of ETFs that might fit into the asset allocation categories for an initial investment of $7,000.

Asset Class	ETF	Ticker
Domestic equity	SPDR S&P 500 ETF	SPY
Domestic fixed income	IShares Lehman Credit Bond Fund	CFT
	Vanguard Total Bond Market ETF	BND
International equity	IShares MSCI EAFE Index Fund	EFA
Emerging market	IShares MSCI Emerging Markets Index	EEM
Gold	IShares COMEX Gold Trust	IAU
Energy	Vanguard Energy ETF	VDE

Portfolio A:
Aggressive, Intermediate Term

This portfolio assumes an initial investment of $7,000, with an aggressive risk tolerance and intermediate goals.

Asset Allocation Here is a pie chart showing the allocation of this portfolio. Above the pie chart is a table showing the assumptions I am using for this portfolio's future returns.

Asset Allocation and Assumptions

	Return	Standard Deviation	Portfolio Allocation
Domestic Equity	11.00	15.26	50.00
International Equity	13.00	16.39	25.00
Emerging Market	15.00	22.62	5.00
Domestic Fixed Income	5.50	5.85	10.00
Gold & Energy	8.00	21.72	10.00

Gold & Energy 10.00%

Domestic Equity 50.00%

Domestic Fixed Income 10.00%

Emerging Market 5.00%

International Equity 25.00%

Projection of Future Returns and Risk Here we have the famous Monte Carlo simulation as applied to this portfolio. The range represents a probability that the percentages indicated represent 90 percent of all conceivable possibilities. The expected return is represented by the 50th percentile. In this portfolio, it is slightly over 10 percent in all periods.

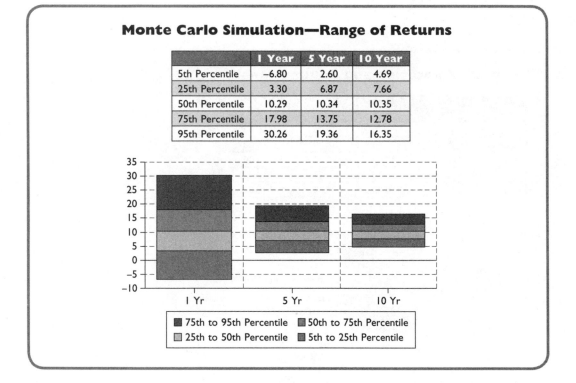

Monte Carlo Simulation—Range of Returns

	1 Year	5 Year	10 Year
5th Percentile	−6.80	2.60	4.69
25th Percentile	3.30	6.87	7.66
50th Percentile	10.29	10.34	10.35
75th Percentile	17.98	13.75	12.78
95th Percentile	30.26	19.36	16.35

Legend:
- 75th to 95th Percentile
- 50th to 75th Percentile
- 25th to 50th Percentile
- 5th to 25th Percentile

This portfolio could lose 6.8 percent of its value in any given year. However, over any 10-year period, the worst case (5th percentile) shows an annualized return of 4.69 percent rising to a best-case annualized return of over 16 percent at the 95th percentile.

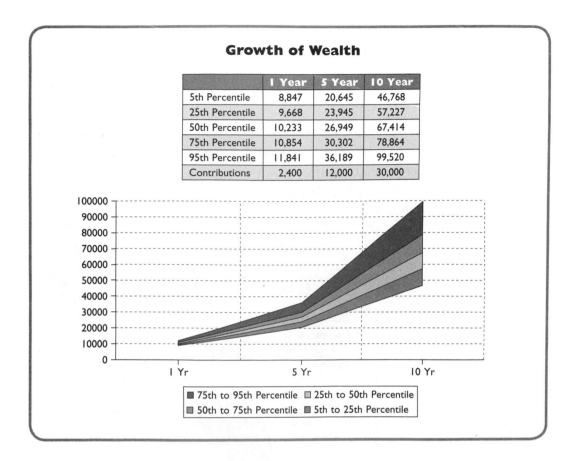

Growth of Wealth

	1 Year	5 Year	10 Year
5th Percentile	8,847	20,645	46,768
25th Percentile	9,668	23,945	57,227
50th Percentile	10,233	26,949	67,414
75th Percentile	10,854	30,302	78,864
95th Percentile	11,841	36,189	99,520
Contributions	2,400	12,000	30,000

Legend:
- 75th to 95th Percentile
- 50th to 75th Percentile
- 25th to 50th Percentile
- 5th to 25th Percentile

In this chart, we show you the growth of your assets over time. Since this is an intermediate-term portfolio, you will likely be interested in the 10-year returns.

Note that over 10 years, your initial $7,000, along with the contributions, would most likely grow to about $67,000.

Portfolio B:
Aggressive, Long Term

This portfolio assumes an initial investment of $7,000, with an aggressive risk tolerance and long-term goals.

Asset Allocation Here is a pie chart showing the allocation of this portfolio. Above the pie chart is a table showing the assumptions I am using for this portfolio's future returns.

Asset Allocation and Assumptions

	Return	Standard Deviation	Portfolio Allocation
Domestic Equity	11.00	15.26	50.00
International Equity	13.00	16.39	30.00
Emerging Market	15.00	22.62	10.00
Domestic Fixed Income	5.50	5.85	0.00
Gold & Energy	8.00	21.72	10.00

Domestic Equity 50.00%

Gold & Energy 10.00%

Emerging Market 10.00%

International Equity 30.00%

Projection of Future Returns and Risk Here is the Monte Carlo simulation as applied to this portfolio. The range represents a probability that the percentages indicated represent 90 percent of all conceivable possibilities. The expected return of this portfolio starts at 10.7 percent and rises to nearly 11 percent over time. The expected return is represented by the 50th percentile.

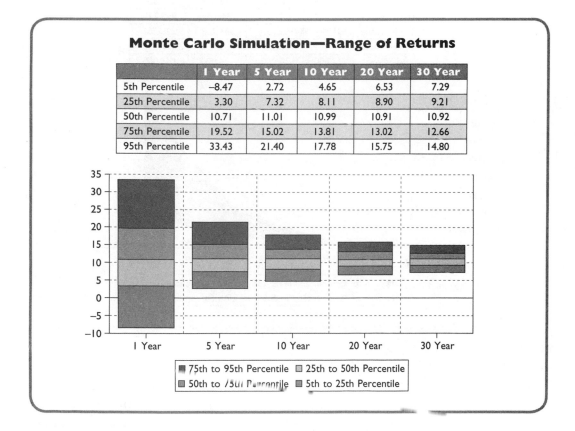

Monte Carlo Simulation—Range of Returns

	1 Year	5 Year	10 Year	20 Year	30 Year
5th Percentile	−8.47	2.72	4.65	6.53	7.29
25th Percentile	3.30	7.32	8.11	8.90	9.21
50th Percentile	10.71	11.01	10.99	10.91	10.92
75th Percentile	19.52	15.02	13.81	13.02	12.66
95th Percentile	33.43	21.40	17.78	15.75	14.80

Legend: ■ 75th to 95th Percentile ▢ 25th to 50th Percentile ▢ 50th to 75th Percentile ■ 5th to 25th Percentile

This portfolio could lose over 8 percent of its value in any given year. However, over a 20-year period, the worst case (5th percentile) shows an annualized return of 6.5 percent rising to a best-case annualized return of 15.7 percent at the 95th percentile. The 30-year results are also good: 7.29 percent at the low 5th percentile and a best-case annualized return of nearly 15 percent at the 95th percentile.

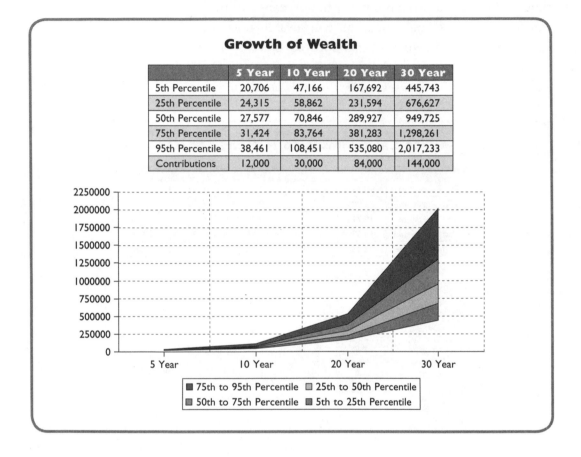

Growth of Wealth

	5 Year	10 Year	20 Year	30 Year
5th Percentile	20,706	47,166	167,692	445,743
25th Percentile	24,315	58,862	231,594	676,627
50th Percentile	27,577	70,846	289,927	949,725
75th Percentile	31,424	83,764	381,283	1,298,261
95th Percentile	38,461	108,451	535,080	2,017,233
Contributions	12,000	30,000	84,000	144,000

In this chart, we show you the growth of your assets over time. Since this is a long-term portfolio, you will likely be interested in the 20-year and 30-year returns.

Note that over 30 years, your initial $7,000, along with the contributions, would most likely to grow to about $950,000.

Imagine! If you start your portfolio while you are in your 20s with as little as $7,000, you could have nearly $1 million dollars before you are even close to retirement.

Portfolio C:
Moderate, Intermediate Term

This portfolio assumes an initial investment of $7,000, with a moderate risk tolerance and intermediate-term goals.

Asset Allocation Here is a pie chart showing the allocation of this portfolio. Above the pie chart is a table showing the assumptions I am using for this portfolio's future returns.

Asset Allocation and Assumptions

	Return	Standard Deviation	Portfolio Allocation
Domestic Equity	11.00	15.26	55.00
International Equity	13.00	16.39	10.00
Emerging Market	15.00	22.62	0.00
Domestic Fixed Income	5.50	5.85	30.00
Gold & Energy	8.00	21.72	5.00

Gold & Energy 5.00%

Domestic Equity 55.00%

Domestic Fixed Income 30.00%

International Equity 10.00%

Projection of Future Returns and Risk Here is the Monte Carlo simulation as applied to this portfolio. The range represents a probability that the percentages indicated represent 90 percent of all conceivable possibilities. The expected return is represented by the 50th percentile. In this portfolio, the return starts at 8.9 percent and rises slightly to 9 percent over time.

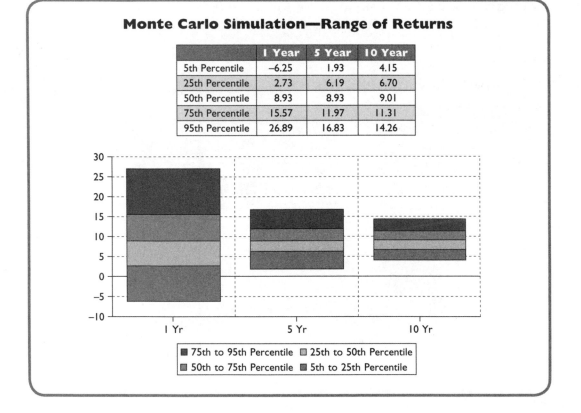

Monte Carlo Simulation—Range of Returns

	1 Year	5 Year	10 Year
5th Percentile	−6.25	1.93	4.15
25th Percentile	2.73	6.19	6.70
50th Percentile	8.93	8.93	9.01
75th Percentile	15.57	11.97	11.31
95th Percentile	26.89	16.83	14.26

■ 75th to 95th Percentile   □ 25th to 50th Percentile
■ 50th to 75th Percentile   ■ 5th to 25th Percentile

This portfolio could lose 6.25 percent of its value in any given year. However, over any 10-year period, the worst case (5th percentile) shows an annualized return of 4.15 percent rising to a best-case annualized return of over 14 percent at the 95th percentile.

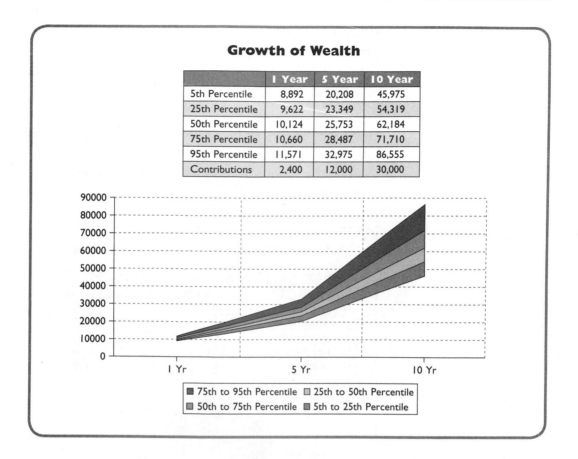

Growth of Wealth

	1 Year	5 Year	10 Year
5th Percentile	8,892	20,208	45,975
25th Percentile	9,622	23,349	54,319
50th Percentile	10,124	25,753	62,184
75th Percentile	10,660	28,487	71,710
95th Percentile	11,571	32,975	86,555
Contributions	2,400	12,000	30,000

■ 75th to 95th Percentile ☐ 25th to 50th Percentile
■ 50th to 75th Percentile ■ 5th to 25th Percentile

In this chart, we show you the growth of your assets over time. Since this is an intermediate-term portfolio, you will likely be interested in the 10-year returns.

Note that over 10 years, your initial $7,000, along with the contributions, would most likely grow to about $62,000.

Portfolio D:
Moderate, Long Term

This portfolio assumes an initial investment of $7,000, with a moderate risk tolerance and long-term goals.

Asset Allocation Here is a pie chart showing the allocation of this portfolio. Above the pie chart is a table showing the assumptions I am using for this portfolio's future returns.

Asset Allocation and Assumptions

	Return	Standard Deviation	Portfolio Allocation
Domestic Equity	11.00	15.26	60.00
International Equity	13.00	16.39	10.00
Emerging Market	15.00	22.62	0.00
Domestic Fixed Income	5.50	5.85	20.00
Gold & Energy	8.00	21.72	10.00

Gold & Energy 10.00%

Domestic Equity 60.00%

Domestic Fixed Income 20.00%

International Equity 10.00%

Projection of Future Returns and Risk Here is the Monte Carlo simulation as applied to this portfolio. The range represents a probability that the percentages indicated represent 90 percent of all conceivable possibilities. The expected return of this portfolio is over 9 percent over time. The expected return is represented by the 50th percentile.

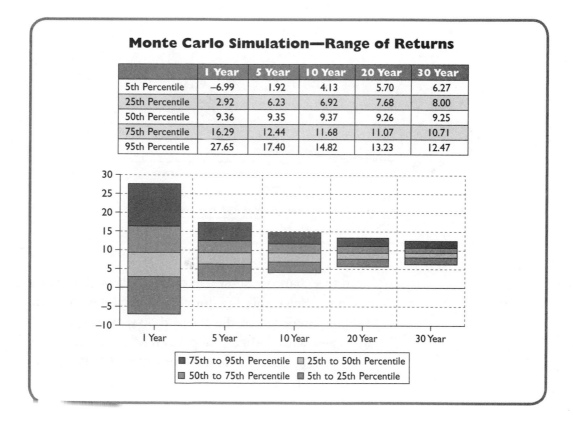

Monte Carlo Simulation—Range of Returns

	1 Year	5 Year	10 Year	20 Year	30 Year
5th Percentile	−6.99	1.92	4.13	5.70	6.27
25th Percentile	2.92	6.23	6.92	7.68	8.00
50th Percentile	9.36	9.35	9.37	9.26	9.25
75th Percentile	16.29	12.44	11.68	11.07	10.71
95th Percentile	27.65	17.40	14.82	13.23	12.47

- 75th to 95th Percentile
- 50th to 75th Percentile
- 25th to 50th Percentile
- 5th to 25th Percentile

This portfolio could lose 7 percent of its value in any given year. However, over a 30-year period, the worst case (5th percentile) shows an annualized return of 6.27 percent rising to a best-case annualized return of about 12.5 percent at the 95th percentile.

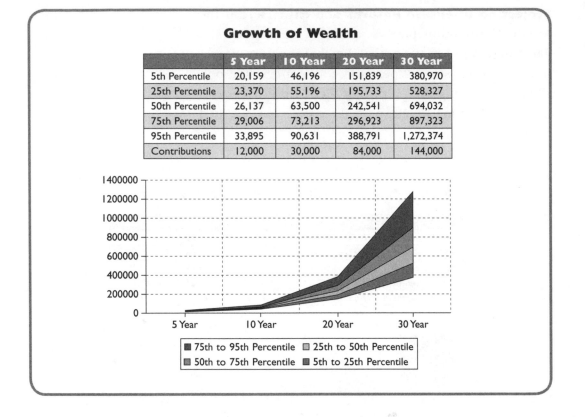

Growth of Wealth

	5 Year	10 Year	20 Year	30 Year
5th Percentile	20,159	46,196	151,839	380,970
25th Percentile	23,370	55,196	195,733	528,327
50th Percentile	26,137	63,500	242,541	694,032
75th Percentile	29,006	73,213	296,923	897,323
95th Percentile	33,895	90,631	388,791	1,272,374
Contributions	12,000	30,000	84,000	144,000

Legend:
- 75th to 95th Percentile
- 50th to 75th Percentile
- 25th to 50th Percentile
- 5th to 25th Percentile

In this chart, we show you the growth of your assets over time. Since this is a long-term portfolio, you will likely be interested in the 20- and 30-year returns, but have a look at the other time periods while you are here.

Note that over 30 years, your initial $7,000, along with the contributions, would most likely grow to about $694,000.

Portfolio E:
Conservative, Intermediate Term

This portfolio assumes an initial investment of $7,000, with a conservative risk tolerance and intermediate-term goals.

Asset Allocation Here is a pie chart showing the allocation of this portfolio. Above the pie chart is a table showing the assumptions I am using for this portfolio's future returns.

Asset Allocation and Assumptions

	Return	Standard Deviation	Portfolio Allocation
Domestic Equity	11.00	15.26	50.00
International Equity	13.00	16.39	0.00
Emerging Market	15.00	22.62	0.00
Domestic Fixed Income	5.50	5.85	50.00
Gold & Energy	8.00	21.72	0.00

Domestic Equity 50.00%

Domestic Fixed Income 50.00%

Projection of Future Returns and Risk Here is the Monte Carlo simulation as applied to this portfolio. The range represents a probability that the percentages indicated represent 90 percent of all conceivable possibilities. The expected return of this portfolio is about 8 percent. The expected return is represented by the 50th percentile.

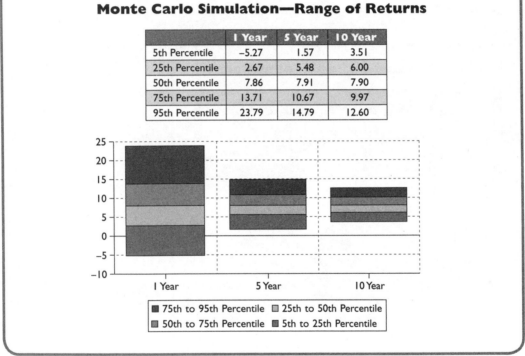

Monte Carlo Simulation—Range of Returns

	I Year	5 Year	10 Year
5th Percentile	−5.27	1.57	3.51
25th Percentile	2.67	5.48	6.00
50th Percentile	7.86	7.91	7.90
75th Percentile	13.71	10.67	9.97
95th Percentile	23.79	14.79	12.60

■ 75th to 95th Percentile ☐ 25th to 50th Percentile
☐ 50th to 75th Percentile ■ 5th to 25th Percentile

This portfolio could lose over 5 percent of its value in any given year. However, over any 10-year period, the worst case (5th percentile) shows an annualized return of 3.5 percent rising to a best-case annualized return of over 12 percent at the 95th percentile.

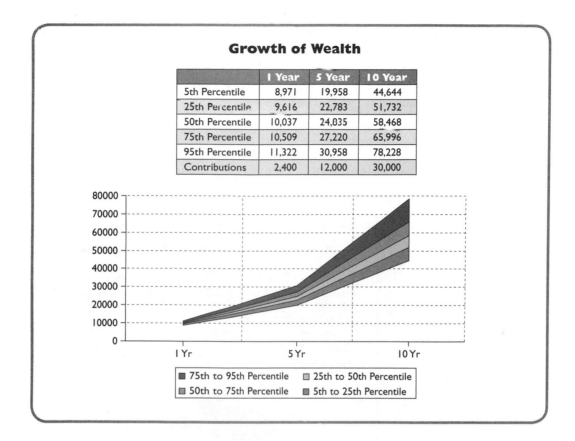

Growth of Wealth

	1 Year	5 Year	10 Year
5th Percentile	8,971	19,958	44,644
25th Percentile	9,616	22,783	51,732
50th Percentile	10,037	24,035	58,468
75th Percentile	10,509	27,220	65,996
95th Percentile	11,322	30,958	78,228
Contributions	2,400	12,000	30,000

This chart shows the growth of your assets over time. Since this is an intermediate-term portfolio, you will likely be interested in the 10-year returns.

Note that over 10 years, your initial $7,000, along with the contributions, would most likely grow to about $58,000.

Portfolio F:
Conservative, Long Term

This portfolio assumes an initial investment of $7,000, with a conservative risk tolerance and long-term goals.

Asset Allocation Here is a pie chart showing the allocation of this portfolio. Above the pie chart is a table showing the assumptions I am using for this portfolio's future returns.

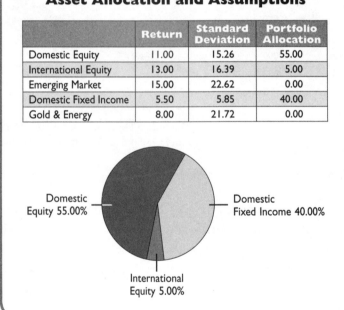

Asset Allocation and Assumptions

	Return	Standard Deviation	Portfolio Allocation
Domestic Equity	11.00	15.26	55.00
International Equity	13.00	16.39	5.00
Emerging Market	15.00	22.62	0.00
Domestic Fixed Income	5.50	5.85	40.00
Gold & Energy	8.00	21.72	0.00

Domestic Equity 55.00%

Domestic Fixed Income 40.00%

International Equity 5.00%

Projection of Future Returns and Risk Here is the Monte Carlo simulation as applied to this portfolio. The range represents a probability that the percentages indicated represent 90 percent of all conceivable possibilities. The expected return of this portfolio is about 8.4 percent. The expected return is represented by the 50th percentile.

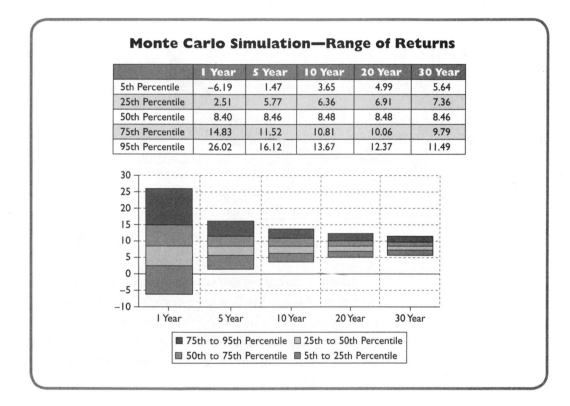

Monte Carlo Simulation—Range of Returns

	1 Year	5 Year	10 Year	20 Year	30 Year
5th Percentile	−6.19	1.47	3.65	4.99	5.64
25th Percentile	2.51	5.77	6.36	6.91	7.36
50th Percentile	8.40	8.46	8.48	8.48	8.46
75th Percentile	14.83	11.52	10.81	10.06	9.79
95th Percentile	26.02	16.12	13.67	12.37	11.49

■ 75th to 95th Percentile   □ 25th to 50th Percentile
■ 50th to 75th Percentile   ■ 5th to 25th Percentile

This portfolio could lose over 6 percent of its value in any given year. However, over a 30-year period, the worst case (5th percentile) shows an annualized return of 5.6 percent rising to a best-case annualized return of 11.5 percent at the 95th percentile.

Growth of Wealth

	5 Year	10 Year	20 Year	30 Year
5th Percentile	20,016	44,739	142,258	339,217
25th Percentile	23,085	52,861	182,757	468,979
50th Percentile	25,322	60,526	220,397	585,771
75th Percentile	28,110	69,503	267,784	753,712
95th Percentile	32,215	83,415	344,563	1,026,094
Contributions	12,000	30,000	84,000	144,000

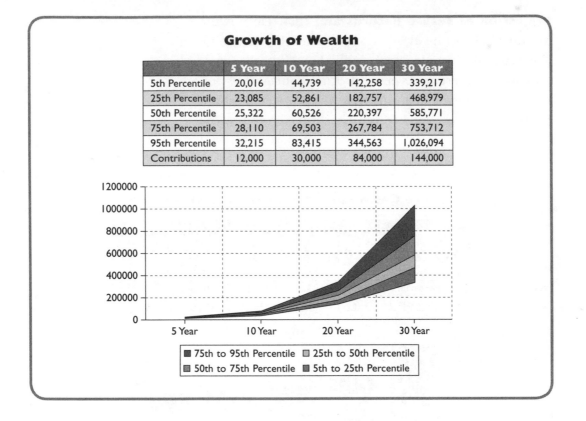

In this chart, we show you the growth of your assets over time. Since this is a long-term portfolio, you will likely be interested in the 20- and 30-year returns.

Note that your initial $7,000, along with the contributions, would most likely grow to about $220,000 over 20 years, and to $585,000 over 30 years.

Starting Level 2:
Initial Investment of $60,000

A portfolio with this initial investment is large enough to use a combination of mutual funds and ETFs. I suggest that for allocations equal to or greater than 10 percent of the portfolio, you select mutual funds for those asset classes. For large-cap domestic equity, I recommend using the Vanguard 500 Index Fund. For the other 10 percent plus categories, I recommend performing a search using the Morningstar screen described in Chapter 5 or another fund screening program.

The return assumptions are based on the history of returns for each of the respective asset classes. In some cases, the historic return has been adjusted to represent the way the current environment has changed. A good example is fixed income and inflation. The historic return for bonds is quite high since it takes into account the very high bond returns of the 1970s and early 1980s when inflation was rampant. I don't think it is prudent to assume that that high level of inflation will return any time soon, therefore I have used a lower number for the future expected return of bonds as well as for inflation.

Standard deviation measures the risk and volatility of the particular asset class. Historic volatility values are also being used here. Remember, the higher the number, the more volatile and riskier the asset class is.

In the chart with the Monte Carlo simulation, you will see the expected return, as well as the range of returns for the portfolio over different time periods. Take a look at what the worst-case scenario, percent-loss would be in any given year (the 5th percentile), and make sure this is in line with your risk tolerance. But always keep in mind that statistically, your portfolio has a 95 percent chance to do *better* than this worst-case scenario, and only a 5 percent chance it could do worse. Also note that as time goes by, the range gap closes *dramatically*. Remember, time is your friend! These statistics should make it easier for you to make an investment decision you can live with.

For portfolios at this starting level, I have also included Alpha charts, which show the likely future performance of the portfolio along with the rising wealth assuming that your active managers or mutual funds outperform their respective benchmarks. For these projections, we have assumed that the active managers have outperformed their indexes over time by 2 percent. Since large cap indexes like the S&P 500 are so hard to beat, we assumed that those allocations would not beat the benchmark. Likewise for fixed income. In this allocation, the Alpha of 2 percent applies to small-cap and international equity components.

The table below shows examples of ETFs that can be used in lieu of mutual funds for the asset allocation categories for an initial investment of $60,000.

Asset Class	ETF	Ticker
Domestic fixed income	IShares Lehman Credit Bond Fund	CFT
	Vanguard Total Bond Market ETF	BND
Gold	IShares COMEX Gold Trust	IAU
Energy	Vanguard Energy ETF	VDE

Portfolio A:
Aggressive, Intermediate Term

This portfolio assumes an initial investment of $60,000, with an aggressive risk tolerance and intermediate-term goals.

Asset Allocation Here is a pie chart showing the allocation of this portfolio. Above the pie chart is a table showing the assumptions I am using for this portfolio's future returns.

Asset Allocation and Assumptions

	Return	Standard Deviation	Portfolio Allocation
Large Cap Domestic Equity	11.00	14.92	30.00
Small Cap Domestic Equity	13.00	19.13	20.00
International Equity	13.00	16.39	25.00
Emerging Market	15.00	22.62	5.00
Domestic Corporate Bonds	6.00	7.30	7.50
Domestic Govt. Bonds	5.00	5.32	2.50
Gold & Energy	8.00	21.72	10.00

Large Cap Domestic Equity 30.00%

Gold & Energy 10.00%

Domestic Govt. Bonds 2.50%

Domestic Corporate Bonds 7.50%

Emerging Market 5.00%

Small Cap Domestic Equity 20.00%

International Equity 25.00%

Projection of Future Returns and Risk Here is the Monte Carlo simulation as applied to this portfolio. The range represents a probability that the percentages indicated represent 90 percent of all conceivable possibilities. The expected return of this portfolio is about 10.5 percent over time. The expected return is represented by the 50th percentile.

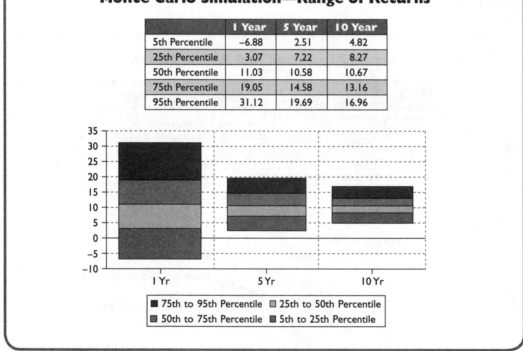

Monte Carlo Simulation—Range of Returns

	1 Year	5 Year	10 Year
5th Percentile	−6.88	2.51	4.82
25th Percentile	3.07	7.22	8.27
50th Percentile	11.03	10.58	10.67
75th Percentile	19.05	14.58	13.16
95th Percentile	31.12	19.69	16.96

Legend: ■ 75th to 95th Percentile □ 25th to 50th Percentile ■ 50th to 75th Percentile ■ 5th to 25th Percentile

This portfolio could lose almost 7 percent of its value in any given year. However, over any 10-year period, the worst case (5th percentile) shows an annualized return of 4.8 percent rising to a best-case annualized return of almost 17 percent at the 95th percentile.

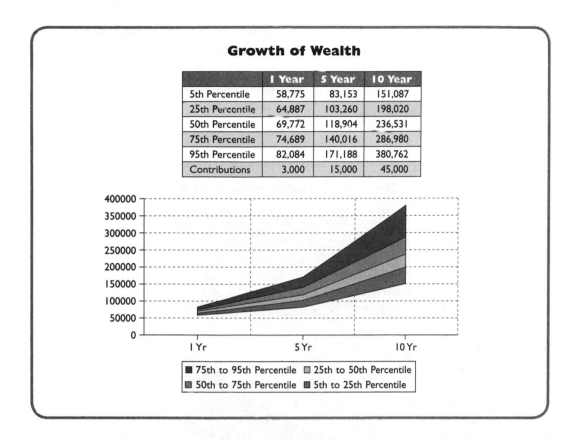

Growth of Wealth

	I Year	5 Year	10 Year
5th Percentile	58,775	83,153	151,087
25th Percentile	64,887	103,260	198,020
50th Percentile	69,772	118,904	236,531
75th Percentile	74,689	140,016	286,980
95th Percentile	82,084	171,188	380,762
Contributions	3,000	15,000	45,000

- 75th to 95th Percentile
- 25th to 50th Percentile
- 50th to 75th Percentile
- 5th to 25th Percentile

In this chart, we show you the growth of your assets over time. Since this is an intermediate-term portfolio, you will likely be interested in the 10-year returns, but have a look at the other time periods while you are at it.

Note that, over 10 years, your initial $60,000, along with the contributions, would most likely grow to about $236,000.

Portfolio A: Aggressive, Intermediate Term with Alpha In this aggressive portfolio, your $60,000 and the additional contributions will probably be worth about $255,000 in 10 years at the 50th percentile. Without the Alpha, or contribution of excess return by the managers, the 10-year figure is about $236,000.

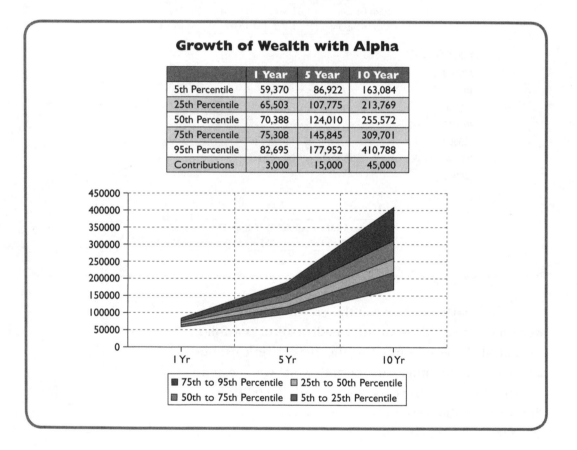

Growth of Wealth with Alpha

	1 Year	5 Year	10 Year
5th Percentile	59,370	86,922	163,084
25th Percentile	65,503	107,775	213,769
50th Percentile	70,388	124,010	255,572
75th Percentile	75,308	145,845	309,701
95th Percentile	82,695	177,952	410,788
Contributions	3,000	15,000	45,000

■ 75th to 95th Percentile   ■ 25th to 50th Percentile
■ 50th to 75th Percentile   ■ 5th to 25th Percentile

Portfolio B:
Aggressive, Long Term

This portfolio assumes an initial investment of $60,000 with an aggressive risk tolerance and long-term goals.

Asset Allocation Here is a pie chart showing the allocation of this portfolio. Above the pie chart is a table showing the assumptions I am using for this portfolio's future returns.

Asset Allocation and Assumptions

	Return	Standard Deviation	Portfolio Allocation
Large Cap Domestic Equity	11.00	14.92	35.00
Small Cap Domestic Equity	13.00	19.13	15.00
International Equity	13.00	16.39	30.00
Emerging Market	15.00	22.62	10.00
Domestic Corporate Bonds	6.00	7.30	0.00
Domestic Govt. Bonds	5.00	5.32	0.00
Gold & Energy	8.00	21.72	10.00

Large Cap Domestic Equity 35.00%
Gold & Energy 10.00%
Emerging Market 10.00%
Small Cap Domestic Equity 15.00%
International Equity 30.00%

Projection of Future Returns and Risk Here is the Monte Carlo simulation as applied to this portfolio. The range represents a probability that the percentages indicated represent 90 percent of all conceivable possibilities. The expected return of this portfolio is a little higher than 11 percent over time. The expected return is represented by the 50th percentile.

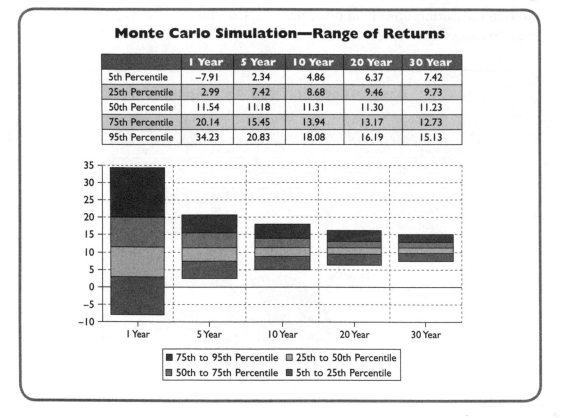

Monte Carlo Simulation—Range of Returns

	1 Year	5 Year	10 Year	20 Year	30 Year
5th Percentile	−7.91	2.34	4.86	6.37	7.42
25th Percentile	2.99	7.42	8.68	9.46	9.73
50th Percentile	11.54	11.18	11.31	11.30	11.23
75th Percentile	20.14	15.45	13.94	13.17	12.73
95th Percentile	34.23	20.83	18.08	16.19	15.13

■ 75th to 95th Percentile   ▨ 25th to 50th Percentile
▨ 50th to 75th Percentile   ■ 5th to 25th Percentile

This portfolio could lose almost 8 percent of its value in any given year. However, over a 30-year period, the worst case (5th percentile) shows an annualized return of 7.4 percent rising to a best-case annualized return of over 15 percent at the 95th percentile.

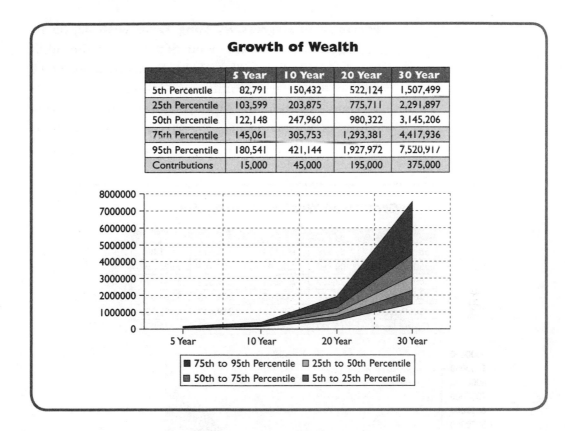

Growth of Wealth

	5 Year	10 Year	20 Year	30 Year
5th Percentile	82,791	150,432	522,124	1,507,499
25th Percentile	103,599	203,875	775,711	2,291,897
50th Percentile	122,148	247,960	980,322	3,145,206
75th Percentile	145,061	305,753	1,293,381	4,417,936
95th Percentile	180,541	421,144	1,927,972	7,520,917
Contributions	15,000	45,000	195,000	375,000

In this chart, we show you the growth of your assets over time. Since this is a long-term portfolio, you will likely be interested in the 20- and 30-year returns, but have a look at the other time periods while you are at it.

Note that your initial $60,000, along with the contributions, will most likely to grow to about $980,000 over 20 years, and over 30 years, you will likely have over $3 million.

Portfolio B: Aggressive, Long Term with Alpha In this aggressive portfolio, your $60,000 and the additional contributions will probably be worth about $1.14 million, and nearly $4 million in 30 years, at the 50th percentile. Without the Alpha, or contribution of excess return by the managers, the 20-year figure is about $980,000, and the 30-year figure is about $3.1 million.

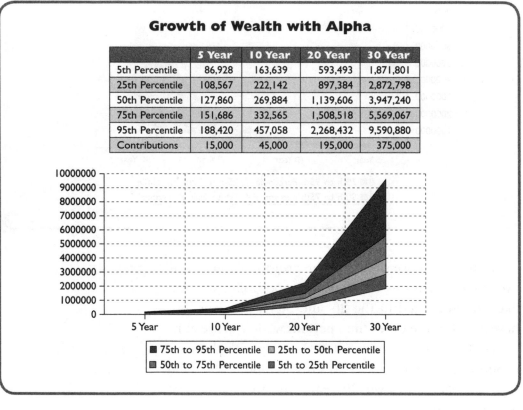

Growth of Wealth with Alpha

	5 Year	10 Year	20 Year	30 Year
5th Percentile	86,928	163,639	593,493	1,871,801
25th Percentile	108,567	222,142	897,384	2,872,798
50th Percentile	127,860	269,884	1,139,606	3,947,240
75th Percentile	151,686	332,565	1,508,518	5,569,067
95th Percentile	188,420	457,058	2,268,432	9,590,880
Contributions	15,000	45,000	195,000	375,000

- 75th to 95th Percentile
- 50th to 75th Percentile
- 25th to 50th Percentile
- 5th to 25th Percentile

Portfolio C:
Moderate Risk, Intermediate Term

This portfolio assumes an initial investment of $60,000 with a moderate risk tolerance and intermediate-term goals.

Asset Allocation Here is a pie chart showing the allocation of this portfolio. Above the pie chart is a table showing the assumptions I am using for this portfolio's future returns.

Asset Allocation and Assumptions

	Return	Standard Deviation	Portfolio Allocation
Large Cap Domestic Equity	11.00	14.92	30.00
Small Cap Domestic Equity	13.00	19.13	25.00
International Equity	13.00	16.39	10.00
Emerging Market	15.00	22.62	0.00
Domestic Corporate Bonds	6.00	7.30	15.00
Domestic Govt. Bonds	5.00	5.32	15.00
Gold & Energy	8.00	21.72	5.00

Large Cap Domestic Equity 30.00%

Gold & Energy 5.00%

Domestic Govt. Bonds 15.00%

Domestic Corporate Bonds 15.00%

International Equity 10.00%

Small Cap Domestic Equity 25.00%

Projection of Future Returns and Risk Here we have the famous Monte Carlo simulation as applied to this portfolio. The range represents a probability that the percentages indicated represent 90 percent of all conceivable possibilities. The expected return of this portfolio is around 9.4 percent over time. The expected return is represented by the 50th percentile.

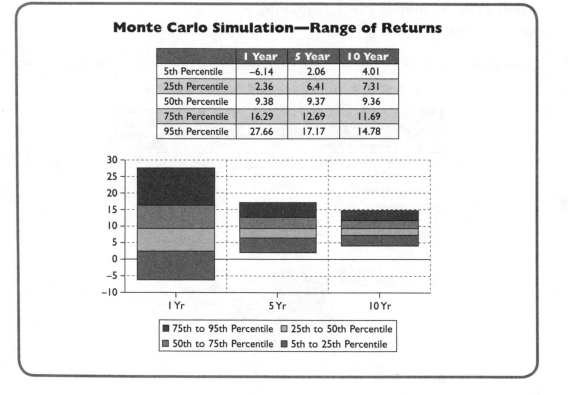

Monte Carlo Simulation—Range of Returns

	1 Year	5 Year	10 Year
5th Percentile	−6.14	2.06	4.01
25th Percentile	2.36	6.41	7.31
50th Percentile	9.38	9.37	9.36
75th Percentile	16.29	12.69	11.69
95th Percentile	27.66	17.17	14.78

■ 75th to 95th Percentile ▨ 25th to 50th Percentile
▨ 50th to 75th Percentile ■ 5th to 25th Percentile

This portfolio could lose 6 percent of its value in any given year. However, over any 10-year period, the worst case (5th percentile) shows an annualized return of 4 percent rising to a best-case annualized return of over 14 percent at the 95th percentile.

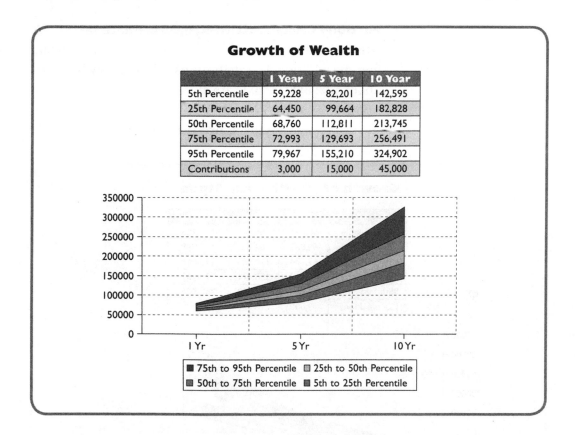

Growth of Wealth

	1 Year	5 Year	10 Year
5th Percentile	59,228	82,201	142,595
25th Percentile	64,450	99,664	182,828
50th Percentile	68,760	112,811	213,745
75th Percentile	72,993	129,693	256,491
95th Percentile	79,967	155,210	324,902
Contributions	3,000	15,000	45,000

Legend:
- 75th to 95th Percentile
- 50th to 75th Percentile
- 25th to 50th Percentile
- 5th to 25th Percentile

In this chart, we show you the growth of your assets over time. Since this is an intermediate-term portfolio, you will likely be interested in the 10 year returns.

Note that over 10 years, your initial $60,000 along with the contributions, would most likely to grow to about $214,000.

Portfolio C: Moderate Risk, Intermediate Term with Alpha In this moderate risk portfolio, your $60,000 and the additional contributions will probably be worth about $225,000 in 10 years at the 50th percentile. Without the Alpha, or contribution of excess return by the managers, the 10-year figure is about $214,000.

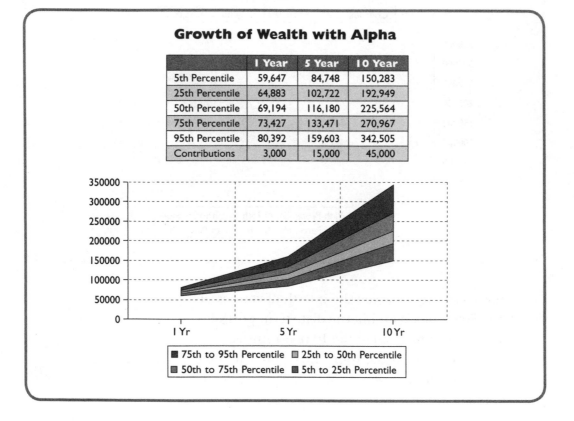

Growth of Wealth with Alpha

	1 Year	5 Year	10 Year
5th Percentile	59,647	84,748	150,283
25th Percentile	64,883	102,722	192,949
50th Percentile	69,194	116,180	225,564
75th Percentile	73,427	133,471	270,967
95th Percentile	80,392	159,603	342,505
Contributions	3,000	15,000	45,000

Legend:
- ■ 75th to 95th Percentile
- ■ 25th to 50th Percentile
- ■ 50th to 75th Percentile
- ■ 5th to 25th Percentile

Portfolio D:
Moderate Risk, Long Term

This portfolio assumes an initial investment of $60,000 with a moderate risk tolerance and long-term goals.

Asset Allocation Here is a pie chart showing the allocation of this portfolio. Above the pie chart is a table showing the assumptions we are using for this portfolio's future returns.

Asset Allocation and Assumptions

	Return	Standard Deviation	Portfolio Allocation
Large Cap Domestic Equity	11.00	14.92	35.00
Small Cap Domestic Equity	13.00	19.13	25.00
International Equity	13.00	16.39	10.00
Emerging Market	15.00	22.62	0.00
Domestic Corporate Bonds	6.00	7.30	15.00
Domestic Govt. Bonds	5.00	5.32	5.00
Gold & Energy	8.00	21.72	10.00

Large Cap Domestic Equity 35.00%

Gold & Energy 10.00%

Domestic Govt. Bonds 5.00%

Domestic Corporate Bonds 15.00%

Small Cap Domestic Equity 25.00%

International Equity 10.00%

Projection of Future Returns and Risk Here is the Monte Carlo simulation as applied to this portfolio. The range represents a probability that the percentages indicated represent 90 percent of all conceivable possibilities. The expected return of this portfolio is close to 10 percent over time. The expected return is represented by the 50th percentile.

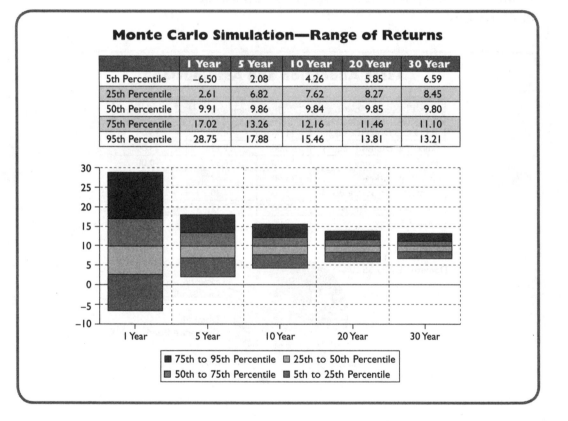

Monte Carlo Simulation—Range of Returns

	1 Year	5 Year	10 Year	20 Year	30 Year
5th Percentile	−6.50	2.08	4.26	5.85	6.59
25th Percentile	2.61	6.82	7.62	8.27	8.45
50th Percentile	9.91	9.86	9.84	9.85	9.80
75th Percentile	17.02	13.26	12.16	11.46	11.10
95th Percentile	28.75	17.88	15.46	13.81	13.21

■ 75th to 95th Percentile ■ 25th to 50th Percentile
■ 50th to 75th Percentile ■ 5th to 25th Percentile

This portfolio could lose 6.5 percent of its value in any given year. However, over any 20-year period, the worst case (5th percentile) shows an annualized return of 5.85 percent rising to a best-case annualized return of nearly 14 percent at the 95th percentile. Over 30 years, the 5th percentile (worst case) would give us an annualized return of better than 6.5 percent and the best case 13.2 percent.

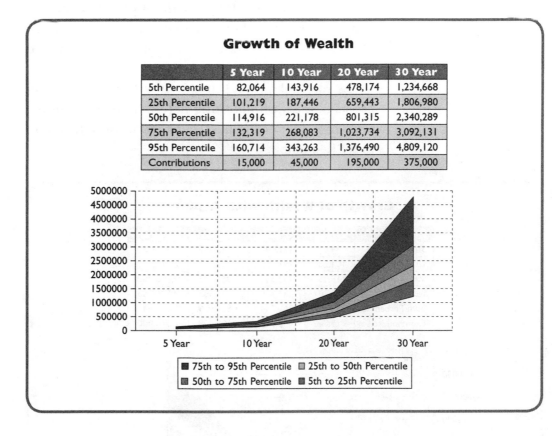

Growth of Wealth

	5 Year	10 Year	20 Year	30 Year
5th Percentile	82,064	143,916	478,174	1,234,668
25th Percentile	101,219	187,446	659,443	1,806,980
50th Percentile	114,916	221,178	801,315	2,340,289
75th Percentile	132,319	268,083	1,023,734	3,092,131
95th Percentile	160,714	343,263	1,376,490	4,809,120
Contributions	15,000	45,000	195,000	375,000

- 75th to 95th Percentile
- 25th to 50th Percentile
- 50th to 75th Percentile
- 5th to 25th Percentile

In this chart, we show you the growth of your assets over time. Since this is a long-term portfolio, you will likely be interested in the 20- and 30 year returns, but have a look at the results for the other time periods while you're here.

Note that over 20 years, your initial $60,000, along with the contributions, would most likely grow to about $800,000, and over 30 years, to $2.3 million.

Portfolio D: Moderate Risk, Long Term with Alpha
In this moderate risk portfolio, your $60,000 and the additional contributions will probably be worth about $880,000 in 20 years. Without the Alpha, or contribution of excess return by the managers, the 20-year figure is about $800,000. Over 30 years, your portfolio should grow to about $2.7 million.

As you look around at the other time frames and probabilities, it is interesting here to notice that in the worst case 5th percentile over 30 years, you still end up with $1.4 million.

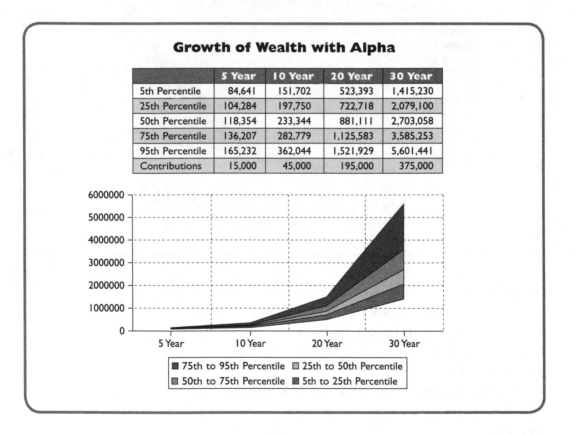

Growth of Wealth with Alpha

	5 Year	10 Year	20 Year	30 Year
5th Percentile	84,641	151,702	523,393	1,415,230
25th Percentile	104,284	197,750	722,718	2,079,100
50th Percentile	118,354	233,344	881,111	2,703,058
75th Percentile	136,207	282,779	1,125,583	3,585,253
95th Percentile	165,232	362,044	1,521,929	5,601,441
Contributions	15,000	45,000	195,000	375,000

Legend: 75th to 95th Percentile, 25th to 50th Percentile, 50th to 75th Percentile, 5th to 25th Percentile

Portfolio E:
Conservative, Intermediate Term

This portfolio assumes an initial investment of $60,000 with a conservative risk tolerance and intermediate-term goals.

Asset Allocation Here is a pie chart showing the allocation of this portfolio. Above the pie chart is a table showing the assumptions I am using for this portfolio's future returns.

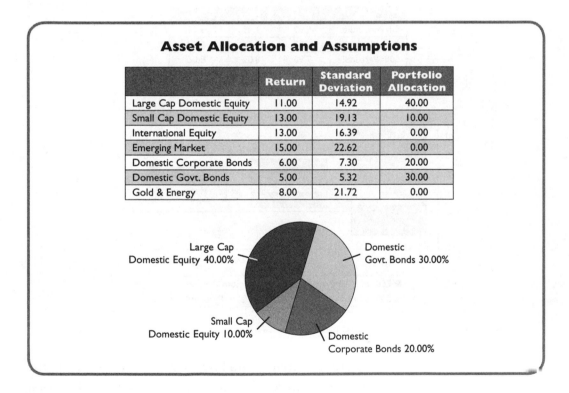

Asset Allocation and Assumptions

	Return	Standard Deviation	Portfolio Allocation
Large Cap Domestic Equity	11.00	14.92	40.00
Small Cap Domestic Equity	13.00	19.13	10.00
International Equity	13.00	16.39	0.00
Emerging Market	15.00	22.62	0.00
Domestic Corporate Bonds	6.00	7.30	20.00
Domestic Govt. Bonds	5.00	5.32	30.00
Gold & Energy	8.00	21.72	0.00

Large Cap
Domestic Equity 40.00%

Domestic
Govt. Bonds 30.00%

Small Cap
Domestic Equity 10.00%

Domestic
Corporate Bonds 20.00%

Projection of Future Returns and Risk Here we have the famous Monte Carlo simulation as applied to this portfolio. The range represents a probability that the percentages indicated represent 90 percent of all conceivable possibilities. The expected return of this portfolio is around 8 percent over time. The expected return is represented by the 50th percentile.

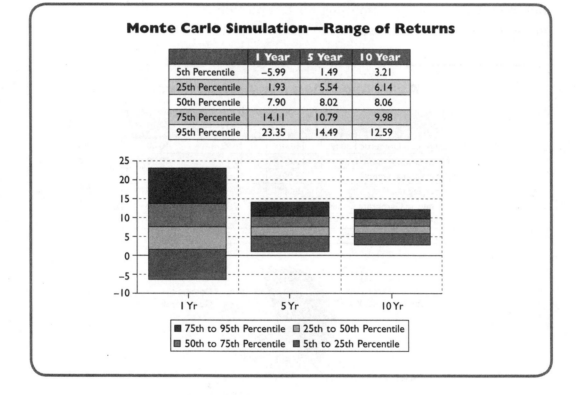

Monte Carlo Simulation—Range of Returns

	1 Year	5 Year	10 Year
5th Percentile	−5.99	1.49	3.21
25th Percentile	1.93	5.54	6.14
50th Percentile	7.90	8.02	8.06
75th Percentile	14.11	10.79	9.98
95th Percentile	23.35	14.49	12.59

■ 75th to 95th Percentile □ 25th to 50th Percentile
■ 50th to 75th Percentile ■ 5th to 25th Percentile

This portfolio could lose 6 percent of its value in any given year. However, over any 10-year period, the worst case (5th percentile) shows an annualized return of 3.2 percent rising to a best-case annualized return of over 12 percent at the 95th percentile.

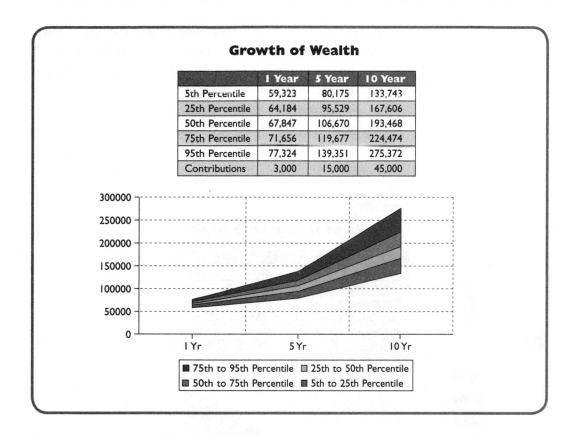

Growth of Wealth

	1 Year	5 Year	10 Year
5th Percentile	59,323	80,175	133,743
25th Percentile	64,184	95,529	167,606
50th Percentile	67,847	106,670	193,468
75th Percentile	71,656	119,677	224,474
95th Percentile	77,324	139,351	275,372
Contributions	3,000	15,000	45,000

Legend: ■ 75th to 95th Percentile □ 25th to 50th Percentile ■ 50th to 75th Percentile ■ 5th to 25th Percentile

In this chart, we show you the growth of your assets over time. Since this is an intermediate-term portfolio, you will likely be interested in the 10-year returns.

Note that over 10 years, your initial $60,000, along with the contributions, would most likely grow to about $193,000.

Portfolio E: Conservative, Intermediate Term with Alpha In this conservative portfolio, your $60,000 and the additional contributions will probably be worth about $196,000 in 10 years. Without the Alpha, or contribution of excess return by the managers, the 10-year figure is about $193,000. This isn't much of a difference but then again, it is only a 10-year investment and only one asset class is involved in the extra return.

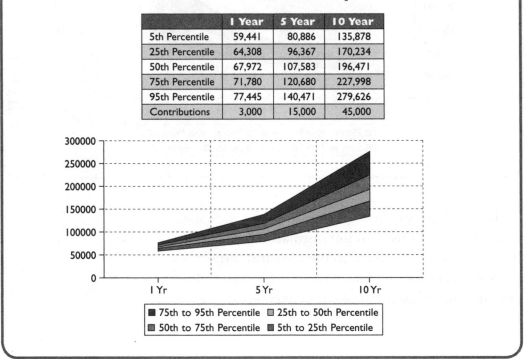

Growth of Wealth with Alpha

	1 Year	5 Year	10 Year
5th Percentile	59,441	80,886	135,878
25th Percentile	64,308	96,367	170,234
50th Percentile	67,972	107,583	196,471
75th Percentile	71,780	120,680	227,998
95th Percentile	77,445	140,471	279,626
Contributions	3,000	15,000	45,000

Legend:
- 75th to 95th Percentile
- 50th to 75th Percentile
- 25th to 50th Percentile
- 5th to 25th Percentile

Portfolio F:
Conservative, Long Term

This portfolio assumes an initial investment of $60,000 with a conservative risk tolerance and long-term goals.

Asset Allocation Here is a pie chart showing the allocation of this portfolio. Above the pie chart is a table showing the assumptions we are using for this portfolio's future returns.

Asset Allocation and Assumptions

	Return	Standard Deviation	Portfolio Allocation
Large Cap Domestic Equity	11.00	14.92	30.00
Small Cap Domestic Equity	13.00	19.13	20.00
International Equity	13.00	16.39	5.00
Emerging Market	15.00	22.62	0.00
Domestic Corporate Bonds	6.00	7.30	25.00
Domestic Govt. Bonds	5.00	5.32	20.00
Gold & Energy	8.00	21.72	0.00

Large Cap Domestic Equity 30.00%

Domestic Govt. Bonds 20.00%

Domestic Corporate Bonds 25.00%

Small Cap Domestic Equity 20.00%

International Equity 5.00%

Projection of Future Returns and Risk Here we have the famous Monte Carlo simulation as applied to this portfolio. The range represents a probability that the percentages indicated represent 90 percent of all conceivable possibilities. The expected return of this portfolio is about 8.6 percent over both 20-year and 30-year time periods. The expected return is represented by the 50th percentile.

Monte Carlo Simulation—Range of Returns

	I Year	5 Year	10 Year	20 Year	30 Year
5th Percentile	−5.92	1.68	3.66	5.16	5.88
25th Percentile	2.02	5.76	6.61	7.32	7.43
50th Percentile	8.62	8.61	8.57	8.59	8.64
75th Percentile	15.28	11.56	10.59	9.97	9.75
95th Percentile	25.29	15.78	13.49	12.17	11.44

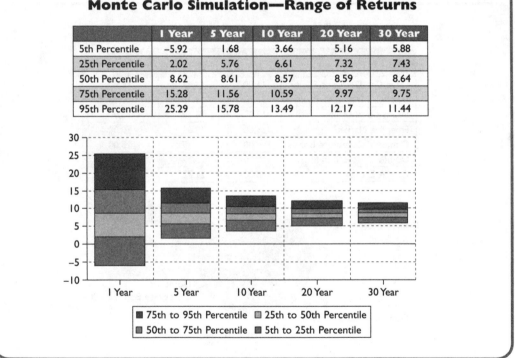

■ 75th to 95th Percentile ▢ 25th to 50th Percentile
■ 50th to 75th Percentile ■ 5th to 25th Percentile

This portfolio could lose nearly 6 percent of its value in any given year. However, over any 20-year period, the worst case (5th percentile) shows an annualized return of about 5.2 percent rising to a best-case annualized return of 12 percent at the 95th percentile. Over

30 years, the worst case (5th percentile) is 5.88 percent and the best-case annualized return is 11.4 percent.

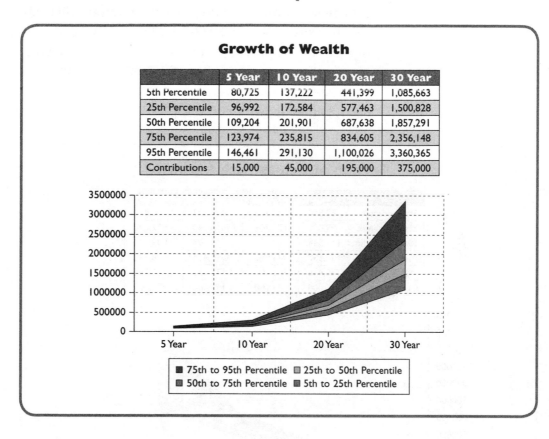

Growth of Wealth

	5 Year	10 Year	20 Year	30 Year
5th Percentile	80,725	137,222	441,399	1,085,663
25th Percentile	96,992	172,584	577,463	1,500,828
50th Percentile	109,204	201,901	687,638	1,857,291
75th Percentile	123,974	235,815	834,605	2,356,148
95th Percentile	146,461	291,130	1,100,026	3,360,365
Contributions	15,000	45,000	195,000	375,000

■ 75th to 95th Percentile ■ 25th to 50th Percentile
■ 50th to 75th Percentile ■ 5th to 25th Percentile

In this chart, we show you the growth of your assets over time. Since this is a long term portfolio, you will likely be interested in the 20- and 30-year returns.

Note that over 20 years, your initial $60,000, along with the contributions, would most likely grow to about $687,000. Over 30 years, in the 50th percentile, you end up with $1.85 million.

Portfolio F: Conservative, Long Term with Alpha

In this conservative portfolio at the 50th percentile, your $60,000 and the additional contributions will probably be worth about $732,000 in 20 years. Without the Alpha, or contribution of excess return by the managers, the 20-year figure is about $687,000. Over 30 years, your expected wealth rises to over $2 million, compared to $1.85 million without the Alpha.

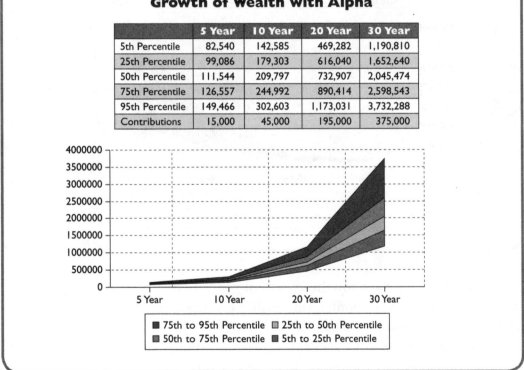

Growth of Wealth with Alpha

	5 Year	10 Year	20 Year	30 Year
5th Percentile	82,540	142,585	469,282	1,190,810
25th Percentile	99,086	179,303	616,040	1,652,640
50th Percentile	111,544	209,797	732,907	2,045,474
75th Percentile	126,557	244,992	890,414	2,598,543
95th Percentile	149,466	302,603	1,173,031	3,732,288
Contributions	15,000	45,000	195,000	375,000

Legend: ■ 75th to 95th Percentile □ 25th to 50th Percentile ■ 50th to 75th Percentile ■ 5th to 25th Percentile

Starting Level 3: Initial Investment of $250,000

This portfolio is large enough to use a combination of mutual funds and ETFs. ETFs can be bought the same way stocks are bought, through a broker, preferably online.

I suggest that for allocations equal to or greater than 10 percent of the portfolio, you select mutual funds for those asset classes. This portfolio has few allocations smaller than 10 percent, so it can be populated almost entirely with mutual funds or you can use a combination of both funds and ETFs. For large cap domestic equity, I recommend using the Vanguard 500 Index Fund or you can use specific large-cap growth and large-cap value index funds. For the other categories, I recommend performing a search using the Morningstar screen described in Chapter 5 or another fund screening program.

The return assumptions are based on the history of returns for each of the respective asset classes. In some cases, the historic return has been adjusted to represent the way the current environment has changed. A good example is fixed income and inflation. The historic return for bonds is quite high since it takes into account the very high bond returns of the 1970s and early 1980s when inflation was rampant. I don't think it is prudent to assume that that high level of inflation will return any time soon, therefore we have used a lower number for the future expected return of bonds as well as for inflation.

Standard deviation measures the risk and volatility of the particular asset class. Historic volatility values are also being used here. Remember, the higher the number, the more volatile and riskier the asset class is.

In the chart with the Monte Carlo simulation, you will see the expected return, as well as the range of returns for the portfolio over different time periods. Take a look at what the worst-case scenario, percent-loss would be in any given year (the 5th percentile), and make sure this is in line with your risk tolerance. But always keep in mind that statistically, your portfolio has a 95 percent chance to do *better* than this worst-case scenario, and only a 5 percent chance it could do worse. Also note that as time goes by, the range gap closes *dramatically*. Remember, time is your friend! These statistics should make it easier for you to make an investment decision you can live with.

For portfolios at this starting level, I have also included Alpha charts, which show the likely future performance of the portfolio along with the rising wealth assuming that your active managers or mutual funds outperform their respective benchmarks. For these projections, we have assumed that the active managers have outperformed their indexes over time by 2 percent. Since large-cap indexes like the S&P 500 are so hard to beat, we assumed that those allocations would not beat the benchmark. Likewise for fixed income. In this allocation, the Alpha of 2 percent applies to small-cap and international-equity components.

The table below shows examples of ETFs that can be used in lieu of mutual funds for the asset allocation categories for an initial investment of $250,000.

Asset Class	ETF	Ticker
Domestic fixed income	IShares Lehman Credit Bond Fund	CFT
	Vanguard Total Bond Market ETF	BND
Gold	IShares COMEX Gold Trust	IAU
Energy	Vanguard Energy ETF	VDE

Portfolio A:
Aggressive, Intermediate Term

This portfolio assumes an initial investment of $250,000 with an aggressive risk tolerance and intermediate-term goals.

Asset Allocation Here is a pie chart showing the allocation of this portfolio. Above the pie chart is a table showing the assumptions I am using for this portfolio's future returns.

Asset Allocation and Assumptions

	Return	Standard Deviation	Portfolio Allocation
Domestic Large Cap Value	11.50	13.86	20.00
Domestic Large Cap Growth	10.50	17.45	10.00
Domestic Small Cap Value	14.00	16.11	10.00
Domestic Small Cap Growth	12.50	23.18	10.00
Int'l Large Cap Value	14.00	16.32	10.00
Int'l Large Cap Growth	11.50	17.30	10.00
Int'l Small Cap	14.50	15.18	5.00
Emerging Market	15.00	22.62	5.00
Domestic Corporate Bonds	6.00	7.30	7.50
Domestic Govt. Bonds	5.00	5.32	2.50
Gold & Energy	8.00	21.72	10.00

Domestic Large Cap Value 20.00%

Domestic Large Cap Growth 10.00%

Domestic Small Cap Value 10.00%

Domestic Small Cap Growth 10.00%

Int'l Large Cap Value 10.00%

Int'l Large Cap Growth 10.00%

Int'l Small Cap 5.00%

Emerging Market 5.00%

Domestic Corporate Bonds 7.50%

Domestic Govt. Bonds 2.50%

Gold & Energy 10.00%

Projection of Future Returns and Risk Here we have the famous Monte Carlo simulation as applied to this portfolio. The range represents a probability that the percentages indicated represent 90 percent of all conceivable possibilities. The expected return of this portfolio starts at 9.68 percent and rises to 10.6 percent over time. The expected return is represented by the 50th percentile.

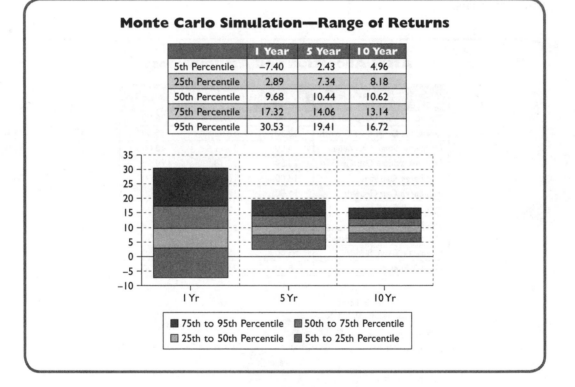

Monte Carlo Simulation—Range of Returns

	I Year	5 Year	10 Year
5th Percentile	−7.40	2.43	4.96
25th Percentile	2.89	7.34	8.18
50th Percentile	9.68	10.44	10.62
75th Percentile	17.32	14.06	13.14
95th Percentile	30.53	19.41	16.72

Legend:
- ■ 75th to 95th Percentile
- ■ 50th to 75th Percentile
- □ 25th to 50th Percentile
- ■ 5th to 25th Percentile

This portfolio could lose 7.4 percent of its value in any given year. However, over any 10-year period, the worst case (5th percentile) shows an annualized return of almost 5 percent rising to a best-case annualized return of over 16.7 percent at the 95th percentile.

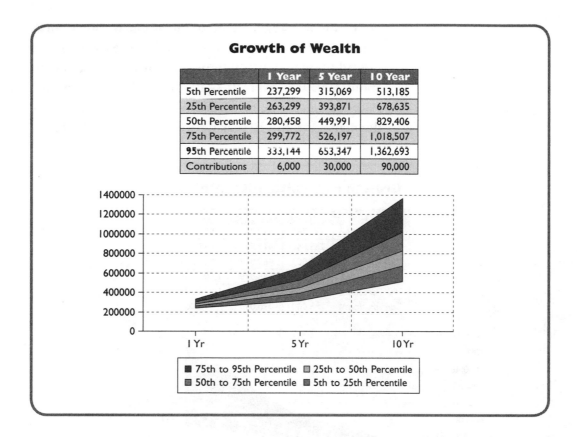

Growth of Wealth

	I Year	5 Year	10 Year
5th Percentile	237,299	315,069	513,185
25th Percentile	263,299	393,871	678,635
50th Percentile	280,458	449,991	829,406
75th Percentile	299,772	526,197	1,018,507
95th Percentile	333,144	653,347	1,362,693
Contributions	6,000	30,000	90,000

■ 75th to 95th Percentile ■ 25th to 50th Percentile
■ 50th to 75th Percentile ■ 5th to 25th Percentile

In this chart, we show you the growth of your assets over time. Since this is an intermediate-term portfolio, you will likely be interested in the 10-year returns.

Note that over 10 years, your initial $250,000, along with the contributions, would most likely grow to about $829,000. Have a look at the other time periods while you are at it.

Portfolio A: Aggressive, Intermediate Term with Alpha In this aggressive portfolio, your $250,000 and the additional contributions will probably be worth about $901,000 over 10 years at the 50th percentile. Without the Alpha, or contribution of excess return by the managers, the 10-year figure is about $829,000.

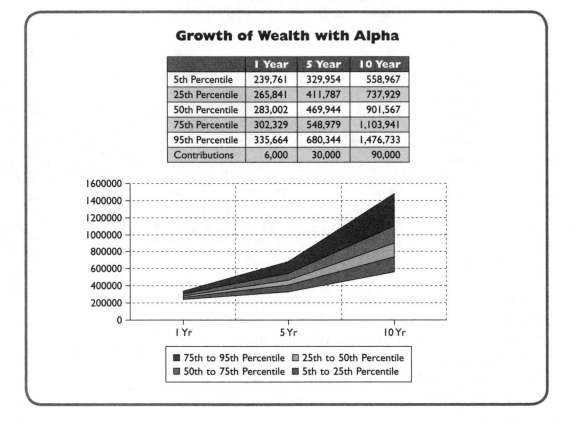

Growth of Wealth with Alpha

	1 Year	5 Year	10 Year
5th Percentile	239,761	329,954	558,967
25th Percentile	265,841	411,787	737,929
50th Percentile	283,002	469,944	901,567
75th Percentile	302,329	548,979	1,103,941
95th Percentile	335,664	680,344	1,476,733
Contributions	6,000	30,000	90,000

■ 75th to 95th Percentile ▨ 25th to 50th Percentile
■ 50th to 75th Percentile ■ 5th to 25th Percentile

Portfolio B: Aggressive, Long Term

This portfolio assumes an initial investment of $250,000 with an aggressive risk tolerance and long-term goals.

Asset Allocation Here is a pie chart showing the allocation of this portfolio. Above the pie chart is a table showing the assumptions I am using for this portfolio's future returns.

Asset Allocation and Assumptions

	Return	Standard Deviation	Portfolio Allocation
Domestic Large Cap Value	11.50	13.86	25.00
Domestic Large Cap Growth	10.50	17.45	10.00
Domestic Small Cap Value	14.00	16.11	10.00
Domestic Small Cap Growth	12.50	23.18	5.00
Int'l Large Cap Value	14.00	16.32	15.00
Int'l Large Cap Growth	11.50	17.30	10.00
Int'l Small Cap	14.50	15.18	5.00
Emerging Market	15.00	22.62	10.00
Domestic Corporate Bonds	6.00	7.30	0.00
Domestic Govt. Bonds	5.00	5.32	0.00
Gold & Energy	8.00	21.72	10.00

Domestic Large Cap Value 25.00%
Gold & Energy 10.00%
Domestic Large Cap Growth 10.00%
Emerging Market 10.00%
Domestic Small Cap Value 10.00%
Int'l Small Cap 5.00%
Domestic Small Cap Growth 5.00%
Int'l Large Cap Growth 10.00%
Int'l Large Cap Value 15.00%

Projection of Future Returns and Risk Here we have the famous Monte Carlo simulation as applied to this portfolio. The range represents a probability that the percentages indicated represent 90 percent of all conceivable possibilities. The expected return of this portfolio rises to over 11 percent over time. The expected return is represented by the 50th percentile.

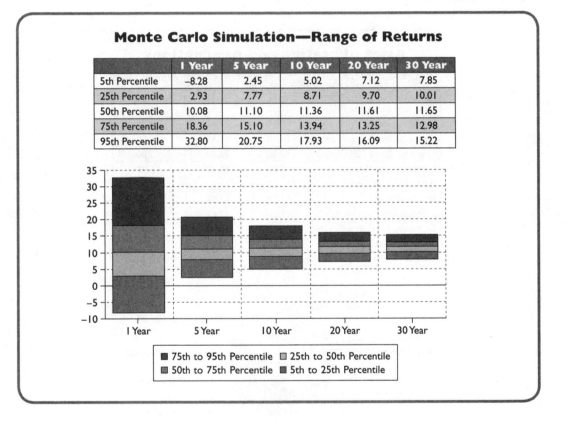

Monte Carlo Simulation—Range of Returns

	I Year	5 Year	10 Year	20 Year	30 Year
5th Percentile	−8.28	2.45	5.02	7.12	7.85
25th Percentile	2.93	7.77	8.71	9.70	10.01
50th Percentile	10.08	11.10	11.36	11.61	11.65
75th Percentile	18.36	15.10	13.94	13.25	12.98
95th Percentile	32.80	20.75	17.93	16.09	15.22

■ 75th to 95th Percentile ☐ 25th to 50th Percentile
■ 50th to 75th Percentile ■ 5th to 25th Percentile

This portfolio could lose 8.3 percent of its value in any given year. However, over a 20-year period, the worst case (5th percentile) shows an annualized return of 7 percent rising to a best-case annualized return of 16 percent at the 95th percentile. Over 30 years, the worst-case annualized return is 7.8 percent and the best case (95th percentile) is 15.2 percent.

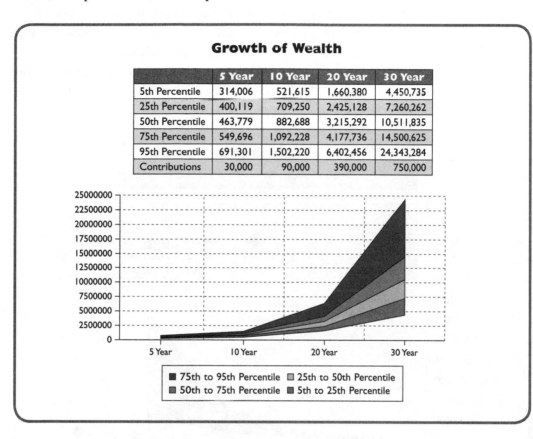

Growth of Wealth

	5 Year	10 Year	20 Year	30 Year
5th Percentile	314,006	521,615	1,660,380	4,450,735
25th Percentile	400,119	709,250	2,425,128	7,260,262
50th Percentile	463,779	882,688	3,215,292	10,511,835
75th Percentile	549,696	1,092,228	4,177,736	14,500,625
95th Percentile	691,301	1,502,220	6,402,456	24,343,284
Contributions	30,000	90,000	390,000	750,000

Legend: 75th to 95th Percentile, 25th to 50th Percentile, 50th to 75th Percentile, 5th to 25th Percentile

In this chart, we show you the growth of your assets over time. Since this is a long-term portfolio, you will likely be interested in the 20- and 30-year returns.

Note that over 20 years, your initial $250,000, along with the contributions, would most likely grow to over $3.2 million.

Over 30 years, you would likely end up with over $10 million! Have a look at the other time periods and percentiles while you are here.

Portfolio B: Aggressive, Long Term with Alpha In this aggressive portfolio, your $250,000 and the additional contributions will probably be worth about $3.8 million in 20 years, and $13.5 million in 30 years. Without the Alpha, or contribution of excess return by the managers, the 20-year figure is about $3.2 million, and $10.5 million over 30 years.

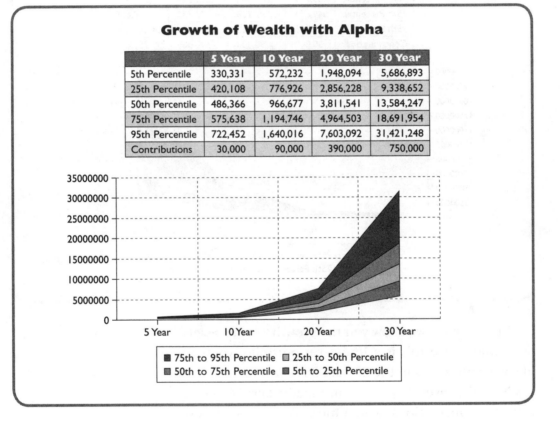

Growth of Wealth with Alpha

	5 Year	10 Year	20 Year	30 Year
5th Percentile	330,331	572,232	1,948,094	5,686,893
25th Percentile	420,108	776,926	2,856,228	9,338,652
50th Percentile	486,366	966,677	3,811,541	13,584,247
75th Percentile	575,638	1,194,746	4,964,503	18,691,954
95th Percentile	722,452	1,640,016	7,603,092	31,421,248
Contributions	30,000	90,000	390,000	750,000

■ 75th to 95th Percentile ☐ 25th to 50th Percentile
■ 50th to 75th Percentile ■ 5th to 25th Percentile

Portfolio C:
Moderate, Intermediate Term

This portfolio assumes an initial investment of $250,000 with a moderate risk tolerance and intermediate-term goals.

Asset Allocation Here is a pie chart showing the allocation of this portfolio. Above the pie chart is a table showing the assumptions I am using for this portfolio's future returns.

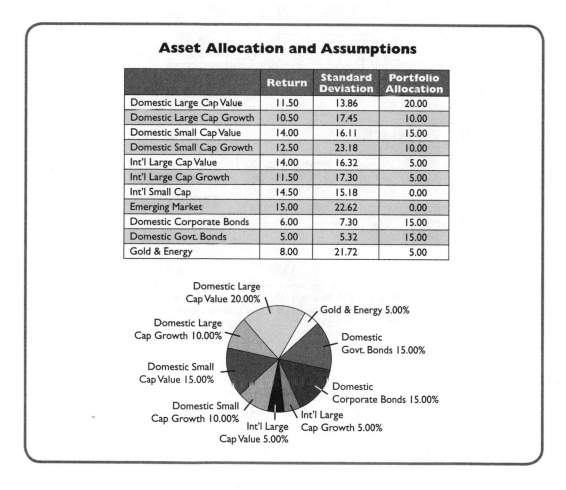

Asset Allocation and Assumptions

	Return	Standard Deviation	Portfolio Allocation
Domestic Large Cap Value	11.50	13.86	20.00
Domestic Large Cap Growth	10.50	17.45	10.00
Domestic Small Cap Value	14.00	16.11	15.00
Domestic Small Cap Growth	12.50	23.18	10.00
Int'l Large Cap Value	14.00	16.32	5.00
Int'l Large Cap Growth	11.50	17.30	5.00
Int'l Small Cap	14.50	15.18	0.00
Emerging Market	15.00	22.62	0.00
Domestic Corporate Bonds	6.00	7.30	15.00
Domestic Govt. Bonds	5.00	5.32	15.00
Gold & Energy	8.00	21.72	5.00

Projection of Future Returns and Risk Here we have the famous Monte Carlo simulation as applied to this portfolio. The range represents a probability that the percentages indicated represent 90 percent of all conceivable possibilities. The expected return of this portfolio starts at around 9 percent and rises a bit over time. The expected return is represented by the 50th percentile.

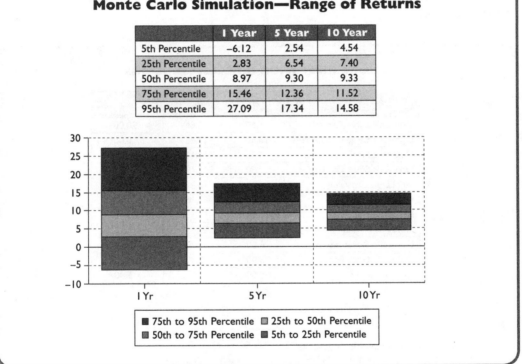

Monte Carlo Simulation—Range of Returns

	I Year	5 Year	10 Year
5th Percentile	−6.12	2.54	4.54
25th Percentile	2.83	6.54	7.40
50th Percentile	8.97	9.30	9.33
75th Percentile	15.46	12.36	11.52
95th Percentile	27.09	17.34	14.58

Legend:
- 75th to 95th Percentile
- 25th to 50th Percentile
- 50th to 75th Percentile
- 5th to 25th Percentile

This portfolio could lose 6 percent of its value in any given year. However, over any 10-year period, the worst case (5th percentile) shows an annualized return of 4.5 percent rising to a best-case annualized return of 14.5 percent at the 95th percentile.

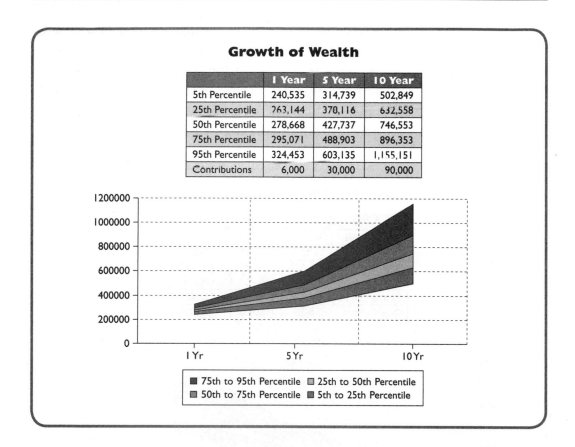

Growth of Wealth

	1 Year	5 Year	10 Year
5th Percentile	240,535	314,739	502,849
25th Percentile	263,144	370,116	632,558
50th Percentile	278,668	427,737	746,553
75th Percentile	295,071	488,903	896,353
95th Percentile	324,453	603,135	1,155,151
Contributions	6,000	30,000	90,000

■ 75th to 95th Percentile ■ 25th to 50th Percentile
■ 50th to 75th Percentile ■ 5th to 25th Percentile

In this chart, we show you the growth of your assets over time. Since this is an intermediate-term portfolio, you will likely be interested in the 10-year returns, but have a look at the other time periods while you are at it.

Note that over 10 years, your initial $250,000, along with the contributions, would most likely grow to about $746,000.

Portfolio C: Moderate, Intermediate Term with Alpha In this moderate risk portfolio, your $250,000 and the additional contributions will probably be worth about $791,000 in 10 years at the 50th percentile. Without the Alpha, or contribution of excess return by the managers, the 10-year figure is about $746,000.

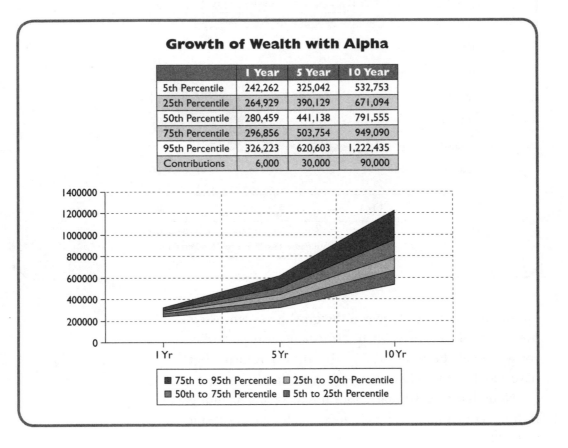

Growth of Wealth with Alpha

	1 Year	5 Year	10 Year
5th Percentile	242,262	325,042	532,753
25th Percentile	264,929	390,129	671,094
50th Percentile	280,459	441,138	791,555
75th Percentile	296,856	503,754	949,090
95th Percentile	326,223	620,603	1,222,435
Contributions	6,000	30,000	90,000

- 75th to 95th Percentile
- 25th to 50th Percentile
- 50th to 75th Percentile
- 5th to 25th Percentile

Portfolio D:
Moderate, Long Term

This portfolio assumes an initial investment of $250,000 with a moderate risk tolerance and long-term goals.

Asset Allocation Here is a pie chart showing the allocation of this portfolio. Above the pie chart is a table showing the assumptions I am using for this portfolio's future returns.

Asset Allocation and Assumptions

	Return	Standard Deviation	Portfolio Allocation
Domestic Large Cap Value	11.50	13.86	25.00
Domestic Large Cap Growth	10.50	17.45	10.00
Domestic Small Cap Value	14.00	16.11	15.00
Domestic Small Cap Growth	12.50	23.18	10.00
Int'l Large Cap Value	14.00	16.32	5.00
Int'l Large Cap Growth	11.50	17.30	5.00
Int'l Small Cap	14.50	15.18	0.00
Emerging Market	15.00	22.62	0.00
Domestic Corporate Bonds	6.00	7.30	15.00
Domestic Govt. Bonds	5.00	5.32	5.00
Gold & Energy	8.00	21.72	10.00

Domestic Large Cap Value 25.00%
Domestic Large Cap Growth 10.00%
Domestic Small Cap Value 15.00%
Domestic Small Cap Growth 10.00%
Int'l Large Cap Value 5.00%
Int'l Large Cap Growth 5.00%
Gold & Energy 10.00%
Domestic Govt. Bonds 5.00%
Domestic Corporate Bonds 15.00%

Projection of Future Returns and Risk Here we have the famous Monte Carlo simulation as applied to this portfolio. The range represents a probability that the percentages indicated represent 90 percent of all conceivable possibilities. The expected return of this portfolio rises to about 10 percent over time. The expected return is represented by the 50th percentile.

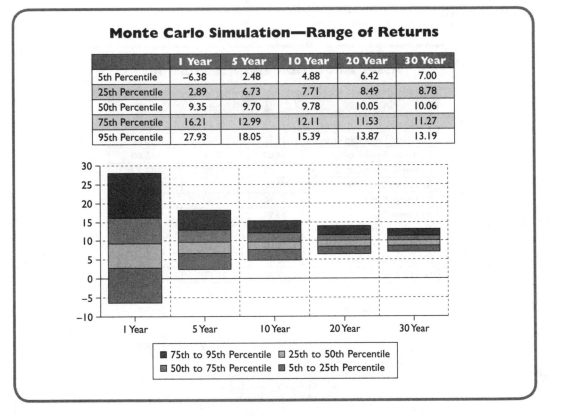

Monte Carlo Simulation—Range of Returns

	I Year	5 Year	10 Year	20 Year	30 Year
5th Percentile	−6.38	2.48	4.88	6.42	7.00
25th Percentile	2.89	6.73	7.71	8.49	8.78
50th Percentile	9.35	9.70	9.78	10.05	10.06
75th Percentile	16.21	12.99	12.11	11.53	11.27
95th Percentile	27.93	18.05	15.39	13.87	13.19

■ 75th to 95th Percentile ☐ 25th to 50th Percentile
☐ 50th to 75th Percentile ■ 5th to 25th Percentile

This portfolio could lose over 6 percent of its value in any given year. However, over any 20-year period, the worst case (5th percentile) shows an annualized return of 6.4 percent rising to a best-case annualized return of nearly 14 percent at the 95th percentile. Over 30 years, the worst-case annualized performance of this portfolio is 7 percent rising to a best case of 13 percent.

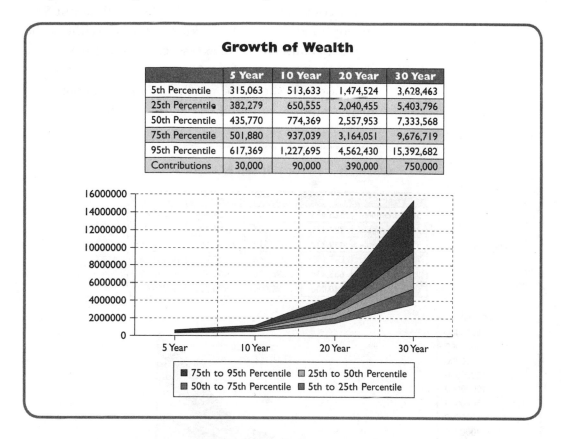

Growth of Wealth

	5 Year	10 Year	20 Year	30 Year
5th Percentile	315,063	513,633	1,474,524	3,628,463
25th Percentile	382,279	650,555	2,040,455	5,403,796
50th Percentile	435,770	774,369	2,557,953	7,333,568
75th Percentile	501,880	937,039	3,164,051	9,676,719
95th Percentile	617,369	1,227,695	4,562,430	15,392,682
Contributions	30,000	90,000	390,000	750,000

■ 75th to 95th Percentile ■ 25th to 50th Percentile
■ 50th to 75th Percentile ■ 5th to 25th Percentile

In this chart, we show you the growth of your assets over time. Since this is a long-term portfolio, you will likely be interested in the 20- and 30-year returns.

Note that over 20 years, your initial $250,000, along with the contributions, would most likely grow to about $2.5 million. Over 30 years, you will likely end up with a tidy nest egg of $7.3 million.

Portfolio D: Moderate, Long Term with Alpha In this moderate risk portfolio, your $250,000 and the additional contributions will probably be worth about $2.8 million in 20 years at the 50th percentile. Without the Alpha, or contribution of excess return by the managers, the 20-year figure is about $2.5 million. Over 30 years, your portfolio should be worth $8.6 million, compared to $7.3 million without the benefit of Alpha.

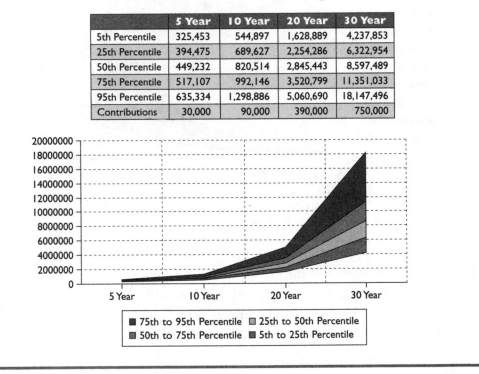

Growth of Wealth with Alpha

	5 Year	10 Year	20 Year	30 Year
5th Percentile	325,453	544,897	1,628,889	4,237,853
25th Percentile	394,475	689,627	2,254,286	6,322,954
50th Percentile	449,232	820,514	2,845,443	8,597,489
75th Percentile	517,107	992,146	3,520,799	11,351,033
95th Percentile	635,334	1,298,886	5,060,690	18,147,496
Contributions	30,000	90,000	390,000	750,000

Legend:
- 75th to 95th Percentile
- 25th to 50th Percentile
- 50th to 75th Percentile
- 5th to 25th Percentile

Portfolio E:
Conservative, Intermediate Term

This portfolio assumes an initial investment of $250,000 with a conservative risk tolerance and intermediate-term goals.

Asset Allocation Here is a pie chart showing the allocation of this portfolio. Above the pie chart is a table showing the assumptions I am using for this portfolio's future returns.

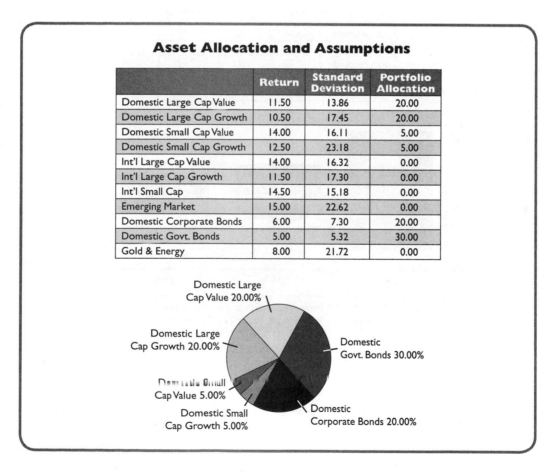

Asset Allocation and Assumptions

	Return	Standard Deviation	Portfolio Allocation
Domestic Large Cap Value	11.50	13.86	20.00
Domestic Large Cap Growth	10.50	17.45	20.00
Domestic Small Cap Value	14.00	16.11	5.00
Domestic Small Cap Growth	12.50	23.18	5.00
Int'l Large Cap Value	14.00	16.32	0.00
Int'l Large Cap Growth	11.50	17.30	0.00
Int'l Small Cap	14.50	15.18	0.00
Emerging Market	15.00	22.62	0.00
Domestic Corporate Bonds	6.00	7.30	20.00
Domestic Govt. Bonds	5.00	5.32	30.00
Gold & Energy	8.00	21.72	0.00

Domestic Large Cap Value 20.00%

Domestic Large Cap Growth 20.00%

Domestic Small Cap Value 5.00%

Domestic Small Cap Growth 5.00%

Domestic Govt. Bonds 30.00%

Domestic Corporate Bonds 20.00%

Projection of Future Returns and Risk Here we have the famous Monte Carlo simulation as applied to this portfolio. The range represents a probability that the percentages indicated represent 90 percent of all conceivable possibilities. The expected return of this portfolio is close to 8 percent over time. The expected return is represented by the 50th percentile.

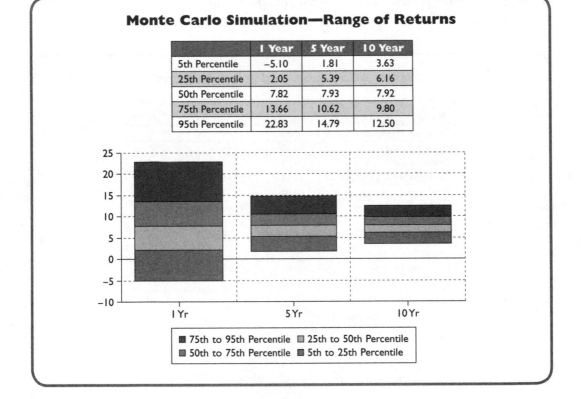

Monte Carlo Simulation—Range of Returns

	1 Year	5 Year	10 Year
5th Percentile	−5.10	1.81	3.63
25th Percentile	2.05	5.39	6.16
50th Percentile	7.82	7.93	7.92
75th Percentile	13.66	10.62	9.80
95th Percentile	22.83	14.79	12.50

Legend:
- 75th to 95th Percentile
- 50th to 75th Percentile
- 25th to 50th Percentile
- 5th to 25th Percentile

This portfolio could lose 5.1 percent of its value in any given year. However, over any 10-year period, the worst case (5th percentile) shows an annualized return of 3.6 percent rising to a best-case annualized return of over 12 percent at the 95th percentile.

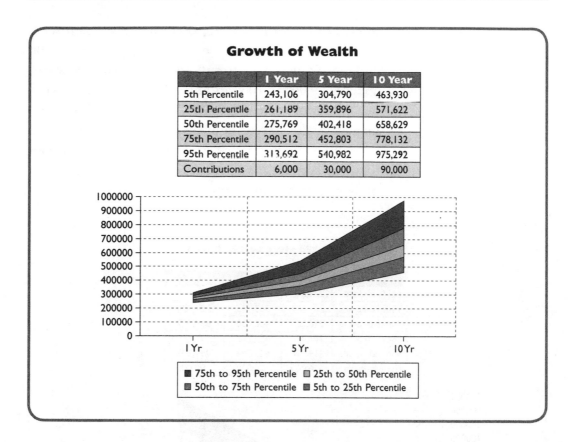

Growth of Wealth

	1 Year	5 Year	10 Year
5th Percentile	243,106	304,790	463,930
25th Percentile	261,189	359,896	571,622
50th Percentile	275,769	402,418	658,629
75th Percentile	290,512	452,803	778,132
95th Percentile	313,692	540,982	975,292
Contributions	6,000	30,000	90,000

■ 75th to 95th Percentile ▨ 25th to 50th Percentile
■ 50th to 75th Percentile ■ 5th to 25th Percentile

In this chart, we show you the growth of your assets over time. Since this is an intermediate-term portfolio, you will likely be interested in the 10-year returns.

Note that over 10 years, your initial $250,000, along with the contributions, would most likely grow to about $659,000.

Portfolio E: Conservative, Intermediate Term with Alpha In this conservative portfolio, your $250,000 and the additional contributions will probably be worth about $669,000 in 10 years at the 50th percentile. Without the Alpha, or contribution of excess return by the managers, the 10-year figure is about $659,000. This is not a dramatic difference since the Alpha only applies to two asset classes and 10 years is not a very long period of time in investment terms.

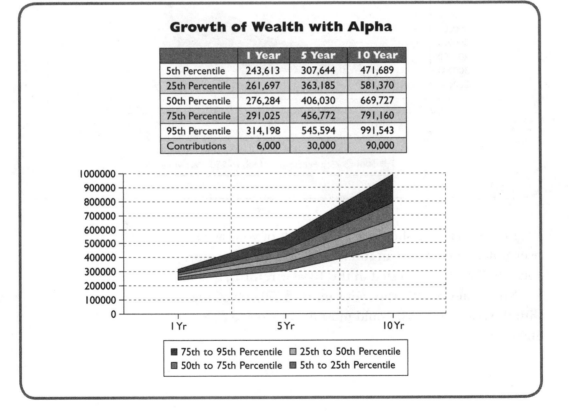

Growth of Wealth with Alpha

	1 Year	5 Year	10 Year
5th Percentile	243,613	307,644	471,689
25th Percentile	261,697	363,185	581,370
50th Percentile	276,284	406,030	669,727
75th Percentile	291,025	456,772	791,160
95th Percentile	314,198	545,594	991,543
Contributions	6,000	30,000	90,000

Legend:
- 75th to 95th Percentile
- 50th to 75th Percentile
- 25th to 50th Percentile
- 5th to 25th Percentile

Portfolio F:
Conservative, Long Term

This portfolio assumes an initial investment of $250,000 with a conservative risk tolerance and long-term goals.

Asset Allocation Here is a pie chart showing the allocation of this portfolio. Above the pie chart is a table showing the assumptions I am using for this portfolio's future returns.

Asset Allocation and Assumptions

	Return	Standard Deviation	Portfolio Allocation
Domestic Large Cap Value	11.50	13.86	20.00
Domestic Large Cap Growth	10.50	17.45	10.00
Domestic Small Cap Value	14.00	16.11	10.00
Domestic Small Cap Growth	12.50	23.18	10.00
Int'l Large Cap Value	14.00	16.32	2.50
Int'l Large Cap Growth	11.50	17.30	2.50
Int'l Small Cap	14.50	15.18	0.00
Emerging Market	15.00	22.62	0.00
Domestic Corporate Bonds	6.00	7.30	25.00
Domestic Govt. Bonds	5.00	5.32	20.00
Gold & Energy	8.00	21.72	0.00

Domestic Large Cap Value 20.00%

Domestic Large Cap Growth 10.00%

Domestic Small Cap Value 10.00%

Domestic Small Cap Growth 10.00%

Int'l Large Cap Value 2.50%

Int'l Large Cap Growth 2.50%

Domestic Govt. Bonds 20.00%

Domestic Corporate Bonds 25.00%

Projection of Future Returns and Risk Here we have the famous Monte Carlo simulation as applied to this portfolio. The range represents a probability that the percentages indicated represent 90 percent of all conceivable possibilities. The expected return of this portfolio is about 8.5 percent over time. The expected return is represented by the 50th percentile.

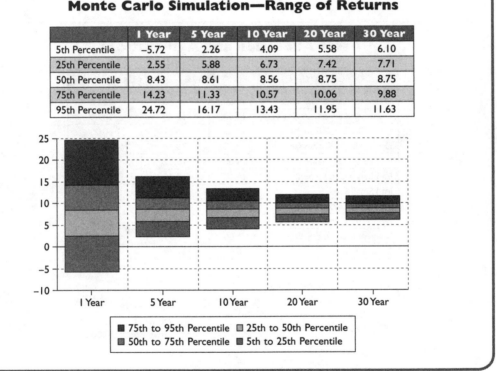

Monte Carlo Simulation—Range of Returns

	1 Year	5 Year	10 Year	20 Year	30 Year
5th Percentile	−5.72	2.26	4.09	5.58	6.10
25th Percentile	2.55	5.88	6.73	7.42	7.71
50th Percentile	8.43	8.61	8.56	8.75	8.75
75th Percentile	14.23	11.33	10.57	10.06	9.88
95th Percentile	24.72	16.17	13.43	11.95	11.63

Legend:
- ■ 75th to 95th Percentile
- □ 25th to 50th Percentile
- ■ 50th to 75th Percentile
- ■ 5th to 25th Percentile

This portfolio could lose 5.7 percent of its value in any given year. However, over any 20-year period, the worst case (5th percentile) shows an annualized return of 5.6 percent rising to a best-case annualized return of nearly 12 percent at the 95th percentile. Over 30 years, the worst case shows an annualized return of 6.1 percent rising to 11.6 percent in the 95th percentile.

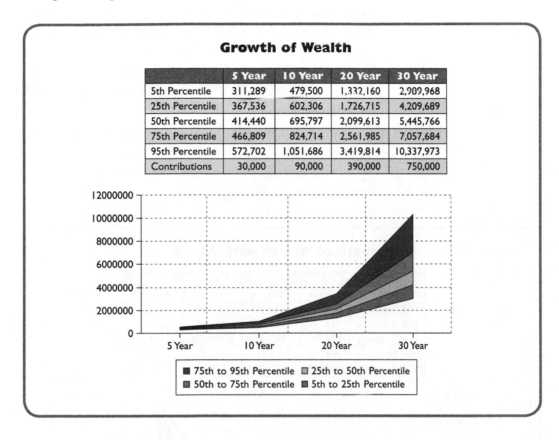

Growth of Wealth

	5 Year	10 Year	20 Year	30 Year
5th Percentile	311,289	479,500	1,332,160	2,909,968
25th Percentile	367,536	602,306	1,726,715	4,209,689
50th Percentile	414,440	695,797	2,099,613	5,445,766
75th Percentile	466,809	824,714	2,561,985	7,057,684
95th Percentile	572,702	1,051,686	3,419,814	10,337,973
Contributions	30,000	90,000	390,000	750,000

In this chart, we show you the growth of your assets over time. Since this is a long-term portfolio, you will likely be interested in the 20- and 30-year returns, but have a look at the other time periods and percentiles while you are here.

Note that over 20 years, your initial $250,000, along with the contributions, would most likely grow to about $2.1 million. Over 30 years, your nest egg should be worth $5.4 million.

Portfolio F: Conservative, Long Term with Alpha
In this conservative portfolio, your $250,000 and the additional contributions will probably be worth about $2.26 million in 20 years at the 50th percentile. Without the Alpha, or contribution of excess return by the managers, the 20-year figure is about $2.1 million. Over 30 years, the portfolio with Alpha is likely to reach $6 million compared with $5.4 million without Alpha.

As you can see, the longer time frame can make a significant difference in the performance of the portfolio as well as a significant improvement in the manager contribution, or Alpha.

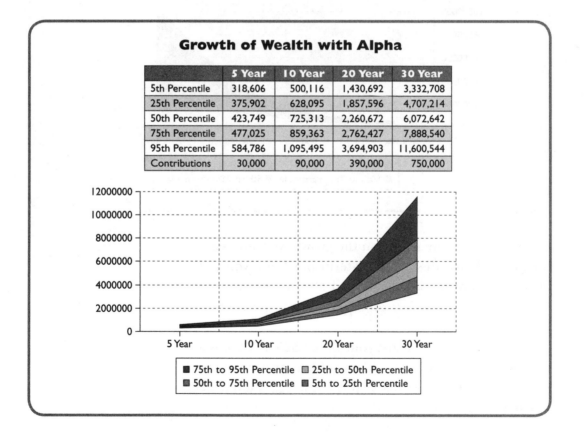

Growth of Wealth with Alpha

	5 Year	10 Year	20 Year	30 Year
5th Percentile	318,606	500,116	1,430,692	3,332,708
25th Percentile	375,902	628,095	1,857,596	4,707,214
50th Percentile	423,749	725,313	2,260,672	6,072,642
75th Percentile	477,025	859,363	2,762,427	7,888,540
95th Percentile	584,786	1,095,495	3,694,903	11,600,544
Contributions	30,000	90,000	390,000	750,000

Legend:
- 75th to 95th Percentile
- 50th to 75th Percentile
- 25th to 50th Percentile
- 5th to 25th Percentile

Measuring Your Winning Portfolio's Performance

By now you have selected your winning portfolio and perhaps it is already populated with your choices of mutual funds, stocks, or managers, and you are on your way to financial independence. As you might expect, you can't now just forget about your portfolio for the next 20 years or so. Much the same as your car or your summer cottage, your portfolio will require a certain amount of maintenance.

Benchmarking

In the investment consulting business, we review portfolios quarterly, checking to see how our money managers and mutual funds are doing. But how are they doing compared to what? To find out, we establish a benchmark—an index or combination of indexes—to measure their performance against. You can do the same, to see whether your mutual fund is doing well, or whether your money manager is doing the job she's being paid to do.

The most important criterion in picking a performance benchmark is that it constitutes a true "apples to apples" comparison. For example, if you have a portfolio

The most important criterion in picking a performance benchmark is that it constitutes a true "apples to apples" comparison.

of small international companies, you shouldn't compare it to the S&P 500, which is a large-cap, domestic index. If you hire a manager to buy small-cap stocks, then you expect him to beat a small-cap index, like the Russell 2000. Why? Because you could buy an index fund that mimics the Russell 2000 index and pay a lot less in fees. So the only reason you are buying a small-cap, actively managed fund, is to make more money over time than if you had simply bought the cheaper index fund.

How will you know if your fund is doing well? You have to check up on it periodically. Here's how we do it:

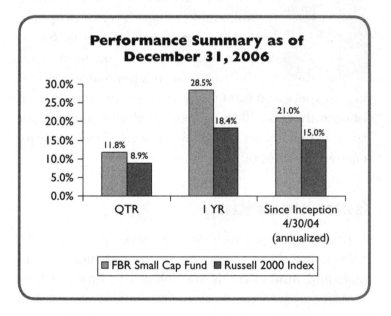

This chart shows a fairly simple bar graph with the performance of the FBR Small Cap Fund compared to the fund's benchmark, in this case the Russell 2000 small-cap index. The first set of bars shows the performance of the fund for the fourth quarter of 2006 compared to the Russell 2000 index benchmark. The second set of bars shows the fund's performance for the full year

2006, again compared to the benchmark performance for the same period. The third set of bars shows the "Since Inception" performance, meaning how well the fund has done since the investor first put money with the fund, in this case, back in April 2004.

Note that the performance in all periods for this fund is very good. In the last quarter of 2006, the FBR Small Cap Fund rose 11.8 percent versus the benchmark Russell 2000's gain of 8.9 percent. For the full year 2006, the fund rose an impressive 28.5 percent, far exceeding the benchmark performance of 18.4 percent. The "Since Inception" performance is annualized from the start of the investment in this fund, and once again, this great fund has risen 21 percent annualized versus the benchmark performance of 15 percent, an impressive performance indeed! (This fund is managed by legendary money manager Chuck Akre.)

If you are comfortable with Excel, you can prepare a simple table like this after inputting the performance of your fund and the performance of the appropriate index over the same period of time. If you don't want to bother, all you need to do to perform the benchmarking function on your own is to pick a starting date, perhaps the first of the month after you bought the particular mutual fund, noting the per share value of the fund on the day you bought it. Then write down the value of the benchmark on the same day.

For example, if you picked a large-cap mutual fund and bought it at, say, $40, and the S&P 500 was at 1480 that day, your objective will be to calculate the gain on your fund from that day forward. Perhaps at monthly or quarterly intervals, check the price of your fund. Look up the value of the S&P 500 on the same day. Calculate the percentage gain of each. If your fund has gone up more than the index, your manager is doing a good

No fund or manager has beaten his benchmark every month or every quarter. Nobody is that good.

GETTING HELP WITH BENCHMARKING

If you have a financial advisor, it is likely that he or she will offer to analyze your funds' performance on a regular basis and that will include benchmarking the funds against the appropriate benchmarks. If your advisor doesn't provide this service automatically, demand it.

If you are investing on your own, check to see if your broker will offer benchmarking services for your fund portfolio. Many do at no extra cost, even the online brokers. Charles Schwab will send investors a monthly performance summary of mutual funds benchmarked against their category performance. Other brokers do the same, although in some cases a minimum account size may apply. It is well worth checking on who might do this important service for you. And it may not cost you a penny.

---

job. If the index went up more than your manager, that's not so good.

When Is It Time to Bail Out of a Fund?

Assuming the fund underperformed the index, now what do you do? Fire the bum? Maybe not. This is one of the most difficult decisions for any investor to make, and also one of the toughest decisions we investment professionals have to make. Look, no fund or manager has beaten his benchmark every month or every quarter. Nobody is that good. That means that if you fired your mutual fund after one quarter of bad performance, you may eventually run out of mutual funds to buy because all of them, at one time or another, will underperform their benchmarks. So you have to approach this with reason and wisdom.

First, by how much did your fund miss? Was the index up 3 percent and your mutual fund was up only 2.5 percent? That's hardly something to be concerned about. That difference is too small for you to draw any conclusions. But what if the mutual fund missed by a lot more? Perhaps your fund manager was up only 0.5 percent compared to 2.5 percent for the index. That would tell me a number of things. First, if the manager is that far off the benchmark, my first instinct would be to examine whether or not we are using the right benchmark for this manager. So we check again. If it turns out the benchmark is the correct one, then the next question is: How concentrated is the fund's portfolio? We know that the S&P 500 has 500 stocks in it. How many stocks does this manager have? If he only has 20 or 30 stocks in his portfolio, then he is going to have a hard time tracking the index exactly. That's because a very good or a very bad performance by only a few of the stocks in his concentrated portfolio will have a very big effect on the performance, good or bad.

The last thing to check in the event of a bad performance is whether or not there have been any major personnel changes at your mutual fund. If your manager left to start a hedge fund or moved to a tropical island with his cute new girlfriend, the fund has to tell you there's been a change, so watch your mail. If you originally bought the fund because of the skill of this particular manager, then you might want to consider dumping this fund. A couple of subsequent bad quarters will make that decision a must.

In the absence of any major and obvious reason for a fund's bad performance, like the departure of a key investment manager, I would recommend you not sell a fund because of poor short-term performance. But if the fund's performance versus the benchmark doesn't improve over the next six months, I recommend you find another similar fund to invest in.

Rebalancing

We've come full circle, and once again we have to talk about that all-important topic—asset allocation. Let's suppose you chose one of the portfolios from Chapter 7 with a moderate risk tolerance that calls for you to allocate 15 percent of your money to small-cap stocks. After a few years, let's assume that small-cap stocks had a terrific run, and this was the best-performing asset class in your winning portfolio. Since small-cap stocks performed so well, they have now earned many more dollars than some of the other investments in your portfolio. When you do the math, you see that your asset allocation in small-cap stocks has increased to 24 percent of your portfolio.

On the other hand, your bond allocation didn't do so well. Interest rates went up, so the value of your bonds went down. You started with a 10 percent allocation to bonds and now it's down to 7 percent. The value of this part of your portfolio went down while the other asset classes were going up.

So now, thanks to the fact that these different asset classes had very different performances over the years, your portfolio allocation is out of whack. The money you made in small caps was so much larger than the earnings of the other parts of the portfolio, like bonds. What do you do? Many experts say rebalance.

Rebalancing is the practice of trimming your investments to get them back to the original asset allocation you selected. Sounds pretty simple, doesn't it? Yet this is a very controversial subject among many investment managers. This is because rebalancing is also a counterintuitive process where you take money away from the winners and give it to the losers. Let me explain. In the example I have been using, your small-cap stocks went from 15 percent of your portfolio to 24 percent based on the large amount of money they made compared to the performance of the other asset classes in your portfolio. That is indeed a winner! Conversely, the bond portion of your portfolio went from 10 percent to 7 percent. Although the bonds didn't *lose* any money, they simply *made less* money than other allocations did. When you add it all up, the smaller amount of dollars in the bond allocation compared to the amount of dollars in the rest of the portfolio means that your bond allocation percentage went down.

Remember that your original asset allocation was chosen based on the important characteristics of each asset class. To rebalance back to your original allocation in this example, you would sell part of the winning small-cap allocation and add some money to the losing bond allocations. You see what I mean about punishing the winners and rewarding the losers? What many investors want to know is whether they really have to rebalance, and if so, how often they should do it. The answer is yes, you should rebalance, but not very often.

First, let's talk about why you should rebalance. Your portfolio was carefully crafted to be the right balance of future reward and risk given your particular circumstances, including your risk tolerance, time horizon, and other factors. It stands to reason that if, say, 15 percent was the right allocation to small caps, then 24 percent is not the right allocation. So to keep the same risk/reward profile you originally decided on, it will be appropriate to rebalance occasionally to the original allocations.

But how often? If your small-cap allocation went from 15 percent to 17 percent of your portfolio and your bond allocation went from 10 percent to 9 percent, should you do anything?

No. The first rule is not to be trigger-happy when it comes to rebalancing your portfolio every time the allocation changes a bit. Some common sense needs to be applied to this rebalancing dilemma. If small caps are doing really well, why not let them continue their run, at least for a while? A small change in the original allocation is not going to have a material effect on your return and risk profile. The best advice I can share with you is to consider rebalancing annually. Even then, only consider rebalancing the asset classes that have seriously deviated from their original allocations by 5 percentage points or more. In other words, if your small-cap allocation was originally 15 percent, I would consider rebalancing only after a change of at least 5 percent (down to 10 percent or up to 20 percent). The same applies to all of the other asset classes in your portfolio.

Summing Up

In this brief chapter, we covered the ways you need to keep track of your portfolio's performance over the years you will be invested. This maintenance activity is important to keep your winning portfolio on the right track to success.

There are two basic actions that need to be performed. One is to make sure that your managers or mutual funds are performing as you expect them to perform. The only way to do this is to benchmark each fund appropriately. You can get help with this, and the best part is that most mutual funds will tell you what they judge themselves against in terms of benchmarks. Check the offering brochure that came with your fund, or if you have one, ask your financial advisor to look it up.

If after a period of time—which I believe should be at least six to nine months—your mutual fund is trailing its benchmark by a significant amount, it may be time to pull the plug. (I'll assume you followed my advice and carefully checked that your original fund was not loaded up with sneaky, expensive fees.) Some funds have early redemption penalties. But you probably will have owned your fund for at least one year before you will need to consider whether or not to fire it, so this shouldn't be a problem. In the event you decide to fire your fund, you will need to find an adequate substitute while remembering to pick one in the same asset class category as the one you are unloading. To do this, review the criteria we talked about in Chapter 5.

The second major activity you need to do is to rebalance your portfolio at regular intervals. Don't be overzealous about rebalancing. This does not need to be done every month or even every quarter. Consider rebalancing every year or so and only rebalance if the original asset allocation is seriously out of whack.

By performing these regular portfolio maintenance activities, you will ensure that your winning portfolio stays a winning portfolio.

Do You Need a Financial Advisor?

Chapter 9

Since I am an investment consultant, you might suspect that I am not exactly an impartial source to answer a question of whether or not you need an investment advisor. It's a little like asking the life insurance salesman if he thinks that life insurance is really a worthwhile product. Well, duh! He thinks life insurance is the greatest invention since sliced bread. So I may have some difficulty convincing you that I am going to give you truly objective advice on this subject. But that is exactly what I intend to do.

There are thousands upon thousands of purveyors of investment advice in the United States. Forgive me, but a lot of them aren't worth a damn. So if you decide you need one, you must be diligent and thorough in your search for the right advisor. But do you need one at all?

For the beginning investor who is starting out with less than $10,000 to invest, I believe that the advice you find in this book should be enough to get you started. You will not need a professional advisor at this point, and to be brutally frank, it is unlikely that you will find one to take you on for that amount of money. Your best alternative for advice at this stage would be

HOW ADVISORS GET PAID IS IMPORTANT

There are a number of ways an investment advisor can get paid. There are three basic payment methods for financial or investment advisors: fee only, commission only, and both fee and commission.

Fee only: The fee-only advisors are paid a fee by you, the client. This adds to your costs because you pay the advisor and you also pay the fees of the investment products, such as mutual funds, that he or she selects for you.

Commission only: The commission-only advisors may well be employees of a fund company or simply independent advisors who recommend funds and other investment products that pay them a fee or commission. Their major sales pitch is that it doesn't cost you anything extra to do business with them because they don't charge a fee beyond what you will pay for the investment products you invest in.

Fee and commission: The combination fee-and-commission advisors have it both ways. They will charge you a fee and will earn a commission on some or all of the investment products they sell to you. The pitch is that they have access to a variety of different investment companies and products and they will pick the very best ones for you. Since some investment companies pay them a commission and some don't, they charge you a fee that is likely to be less than the fee charged by fee-only advisors.

Which type of advisor should you pick? First, let me say that there are very good, honest, professional advisors in all of these categories of investment professionals. Here is my advice: I recommend that if you hire anyone to help you, you hire a fee-only advisor.

Look, it's hard enough to make money and beat the market. So it is better to have an advisor who is not conflicted or restricted in her choice of investment vehicles. An advisor who gets paid by the company whose funds she recommends is more than likely to recommend funds that pay her, and pay her well. Those funds just might be the right funds for you, but why take a chance? If you want impartial, objective advice, hire an advisor who works for you, not for the investment company whose funds she is going to sell.

the large mutual fund companies, such as Fidelity and Vanguard, whose representatives will talk to you on the phone and in some cases offer advice on allocating your portfolio for a modest fee. Problem is that you will only get advice pertaining to their particular mutual fund offerings. But as I said, I don't think you need a great deal of advice starting out with the smaller amounts. The suggestions and direction featured in this book should be enough to start you on a successful and winning portfolio.

As you get richer, however, you might want to rethink your need for advice. With portfolios of $100,000 or more, the asset allocation process becomes more challenging and complex. Although you might be able to do it yourself, you might also decide that you don't want to. In that case, you will need to seek some outside help.

Let's review the various sources for investment advice that you might consider.

Financial Planners

There are thousands of financial planners ready and willing to provide advice to solve all of your financial problems. They range in size from one- or two-person shops to coast-to-coast firms with hundreds of advisors.

Financial planners offer a broader array of services than do most investment professionals. In addition to offering an assortment of mutual funds, financial planners will help you get a mortgage or refinance your existing home, develop a budget to manage your expenses, sell you some insurance, and otherwise offer a one-stop-shopping experience for a wide swath of financial services.

In addition to offering an assortment of mutual funds, financial planners will offer a one-stop-shopping experience for a wide swath of financial services.

Many individuals and families find the services of a financial planner to be very useful. The idea that one person has the answer to all your financial problems is indeed attractive. For people with relatively simple needs, this approach may work well. The problem is that these folks can't be experts at everything. Their investment knowledge will usually be limited and the offering of funds restricted to firms with whom they have fee arrangements. Many of these individuals charge a fee and also get compensation from the funds or other financial products they recommend. That is a big no-no as far as I'm concerned (see sidebar "How Advisors Get Paid Is Important" on page 198).

If you choose to work with a financial planner, pay attention to how the person gets paid. Be skeptical of recommendations when the advisor gets a fee from the company or fund he is recommending.

Financial Advisors

Financial advisors come in all shapes and forms. At the high end are the investment advisors to the very wealthy. This individual might hold a CFA (chartered financial analyst) designation. This is the toughest of the investment industry designations to get. It takes years of study of accounting, financial analysis, securities laws and regulations, modern portfolio theory, and more. It demands the passing of three separate exams at which the pass rate often does not exceed 50 percent. I have a great deal of respect of anyone who holds the CFA designation. Other designations also offer a guide to the advisor's training and education (see sidebar "What Do All Those Letters Mean?" on page 206).

The high-end investment advisors or investment consultants generally accept clients with $500,000 or more to invest. I know of some firms whose minimums are as high as $100 million! Most of the high-end firms are generally compensated by a fee-only arrangement. You pay them to do the investment analysis and they do not get commissions or income from the funds or money managers they recommend to their clients.

Most independent investment advisors, however, are small operations with a dozen or fewer employees and accounts that start at $50,000 or more. They are generally registered both within their home state, and if they have more than a handful of clients, they will also be registered as investment advisors with the Securities and Exchange Commission (SEC) in Washington. The SEC does not pass judgment on the investment advisor's competence; it merely ensures that the advisor files information with the SEC on the form called ADV. It comes in two parts, and part two of the ADV must be made available to every client and prospective client of the investment advisory firm. Investment advisors are also required to pass an exam to be licensed.

A Word or Two about Fees

You may well decide to try a financial planner, financial advisor, or other investment specialist who does not work for one of the large, well-known investment firms. Many of these professionals provide excellent service to clients who would not be particularly attractive to the mega investment firms who are more interested in larger portfolios. These smaller practitioners often provide attentive and reliable service to an individual or family getting started in the investment process.

Of course, this is someone you will have to pay to help you with you financial planning. The fees are sometimes "asset based"—that is, you pay a percentage of the assets the advisor will be helping you to manage.

A fee of 1 percent is pretty typical. Other advisors charge an hourly fee. Some investors prefer that arrangement because they just want help getting started.

But beware: Some advisors either don't charge a fee or charge a reduced fee and also get paid by the companies or funds they recommend. I do not recommend that you use anything but a fee-only advisor (see sidebar "How Advisors Get Paid Is Important" on page 198). Yes, you will have to pay a fee, but you will get objective advice. If you are getting advice from an individual who is getting paid a commission for selling you a particular fund, this person will be selling you a load fund, and if I haven't beaten you over the head enough on this point, allow me to do it again: DO NOT BUY LOAD FUNDS! There are plenty of no-load funds available that have superb records. And I recommend that if you decide that you need investment advice, pay for it and do not get advice from an advisor who is conflicted by virtue of the fact that she gets paid by the companies she is recommending to you.

I hope I have made my point.

Full Service Brokerage Firms

This category includes many of the names that will be familiar to you, such as Smith Barney, Morgan Stanley, Merrill Lynch, UBS, and many others. Most of these firms started out as traditional stockbrokerage outfits and evolved with the times. In the old days, you went to a registered representative—a broker—and he (rarely a she) put together a portfolio for you culled from the stock selections that emanated from their highly paid research analysts. The broker was compensated by commissions he earned on the transactions his client made, so it wasn't too surprising that these portfolios had a lot more turnover than they probably should have had. Much of the old brokerage model has changed. Brokers aren't brokers any more; they are financial consultants and advisors and the like. Their compensation isn't entirely based on commissions but you can be sure that their income is somehow directly related to the revenues they produce.

Wrap Programs and Unified Managed Accounts

Today the brokerage firms even recommend outside money managers who are part of their consulting platforms, referred to in the industry as *wrap* programs. They are called that because these programs wrap all the fees into one flat fee that includes the brokerage commission, the fees to the money managers, custody fees, and, of course, the compensation to your ever-cheerful registered representative.

The wrap programs have some value but you have to negotiate the fee down from what they might want to charge you. These accounts are generally offered to individuals with as little as $10,000 to invest (it varies by firm), and the advantage is that they will offer a diversified portfolio of mutual funds and in some cases access to money managers who generally only accept accounts of $1 million of more. In effect, these managers run a form of pooled funds for the smaller clients of the brokerage firms where they have made arrangements to offer this service. Getting access to these money managers is useful because it allows a relatively smaller portfolio to get the kind of diversification that larger portfolios generally require. That means you can have some money with a growth manager, value manager, an international manager, and others without meeting their minimums for investing directly with them. You might be thinking "Can't I get the same kind of diversification with a mutual fund?" The answer is yes. But there is a certain cachet to getting access to these well-known money managers who normally deal exclusively with the very rich and large institutional investors.

Another benefit of these programs is that the broker (sorry—I meant the financial advisor) will also provide you with a quarterly report with the performance of each of the managers against an appropriate benchmark. As you know from our discussion in Chapter 8, that is a useful feature. If one of the chosen money managers falters, you will be in a position to tell your advisor that you want to replace that manager with another one. And they should be happy to oblige.

A newer version, called UMA (Unified Managed Account), of the all-in-one investment package has emerged and is growing rapidly. These accounts can be considered upscale wrap accounts for investors with over $100,000 to $1 million to invest. Many of the large investment firms are offering, or soon will offer, these accounts. The claimed advantage is that they provide diversification among managers in a wider variety of investment categories including the use of ETFs in constructing a portfolio. Typically, the UMAs use an "overlay" manager to determine the right mix of assets for the client. The overlay manager may be a specialized individual or, for the smaller accounts, a packaged computer program. The client gets the advantage of receiving one statement at the end of the month and one form 1099 for tax purposes.

Costs Some of these wrap programs and UMAs at the large brokerage houses start at 3 percent, which is, frankly, exorbitant. It is tough to make up 3 percent in expenses. That amount will be a huge drag on your performance. With the "smaller" portfolios, which for these programs start at around $100,000 for UMAs and less for wrap accounts, your objective should be to pay something less than 2 percent, which includes all expenses associated with the program. Since the average equity mutual fund has an expense ratio of 1.5 percent, and that doesn't include the cost of trading the stocks, a fee of 2 percent or less is reasonable given that you will get diversification, trading costs covered, quarterly reports, and access to an advisor for a fee that amounts to an incremental 0.5 percent or less over the cost of a typical equity mutual fund.

A Final Note about the Old-Fashioned Way

You might also use one of the large brokerage firms to put together a portfolio of stocks for you, where a broker (who might be called a financial advisor or something similar) calls you and tells you to buy this or that stock and assembles a portfolio for you in that fashion. I really don't recommend this approach unless you are dealing with someone you know very well or who comes highly recommended. The problem here is that most brokers are still compensated by the amount of commissions they generate, and that puts your interests at odds with the interests of the broker. The broker's financial interest is to get you to buy and sell stocks as often as possible. Now he isn't going to do that deliberately, but it is reasonable to assume that if the broker is compensated through commissions he or she earns, this person just might find a very good reason for you to buy and sell stocks more often that you probably should.

WHAT DO ALL THOSE LETTERS MEAN?

So you got a business card from some financial person who had a bunch of initials after his name? What do they mean? Here is an abbreviated list of those initials that you are most likely to come across.

Certified financial planner™ (CFP®): The program is administered by the Certified Financial Planner Board of Standards, Inc. In order to get the CFP designation, candidates must have qualifying work experience in the industry and must pass an exam to demonstrate their knowledge of finance and financial planning.

Chartered financial analyst (CFA®): This designation is offered by the CFA Institute [formerly the Association for Investment Management and Research (AIMR)]. Candidates for the CFA charter must pass three difficult exams and have at least three years of qualifying work experience, among other requirements

Chartered financial consultant (ChFC): Candidates must pass an exam administered by the American College. Requirements include three years' experience in the financial industry. The course of study emphasizes all areas of financial planning.

Certified investment management analyst (CIMA): This designation is offered by the Investment Management Consultants Association and requires three years' experience in the industry. Like the others, an exam must be passed. CIMA designees must also complete continuing education requirements every two years. Most CIMA holders are involved in asset allocation and portfolio management and supervision.

So is any one of these better than the other? All of them represent some degree of professional achievement. The hardest one of these to get, and the one that earns my highest respect, is the CFA designation. It requires passing three separate exams over three years and the tests are very difficult as demonstrated by the high failure rate.

Nevertheless, with the information you have learned in this book, you will be in a position to show that you know what you are talking about when you deal with an investment professional. It changes the landscape, believe me.

Discount Brokerage and Mutual Fund Firms

This category includes Charles Schwab, Fidelity, Vanguard, T. Rowe Price, E*TRADE, and many others. With these folks, we are talking about online or telephonic communications, rarely a face-to face-meeting with a live person.

Many of these firms have specialized services that will help with portfolio construction. Here again, with the benefit of what you have learned from this book, you will be in a better position to analyze the kind of advice you are getting and better prepared for the decisions that you will need to make.

In many cases, these firms will help you put together a portfolio of mutual funds. In the case of the discount brokers, you will have a wide array of choices from many different fund families. Naturally, in the case of the fund companies, your choice will be restricted to their own products, not necessarily a bad thing, just something you should be aware of.

Commercial Banks

Many commercial banks offer investment services directly or through investment subsidiaries. I served on the board of directors of a commercial bank for more than a decade, so here's a little inside scoop. Because there is only a limited amount of money a bank can lend based on its deposits and its capital, commercial banks discovered that the most profitable thing they could do was to generate fee income. That's why banks nickel-and-dime you to death with fees for everything you can possibly imagine, even if these fees are just a dollar or two a shot. The real payoff for the bank is that this fee income isn't limited by capital or deposits; the bank can book as much fee income as it can get its hands on.

Investment products generate fee income so they are a business that banks find very attractive. Every major bank, and smaller ones too, will foist their investment products on their clients with lightning speed. In some cases, these are in-house products and in other cases, the banks, like the brokerage firms, have adopted the consulting model and offer access to funds and money managers who are not part of their own business.

It is likely that you have one or more accounts at a commercial bank, so it is likely that you have been solicited or exposed to the investment products and services offered by your own commercial bank. Here again, you must be particularly wary about in-house products at banks and brokerage firms. These in-house investment offerings, usually mutual funds, are more profitable for the bank or brokerage firm than selling you someone else's fund or services, so you can expect these home products to be at the forefront of the investment pitch.

If you consider a commercial bank's investment service, remember the lessons you've just learned. I'll summarize briefly:

- There is no reason to buy a load fund. A good no-load fund will do the job at less cost.
- Evaluate the performance of any offered investment product against the appropriate benchmark. If the information isn't readily available, demand that information before considering any proffered fund. Don't buy any fund that hasn't outperformed its benchmark over time.
- Carefully check the fund expense ratio and any other fees for reasonableness.

As in other cases, if all else checks out, the last and perhaps most important factor will be the individual who will be assigned as your advisor. Does he or she have the right credentials, experience, and—also important—personality that makes you confident and also comfortable?

Summing Up

In this chapter we raised the question of whether or not you need an investment advisor to help build and manage your winning portfolio. In the early stages of your investment life, when you are starting out with a relatively small amount of money, you may not need professional advice. Later on, as your assets grow, you might want to consider getting some professional help to guide you. We talked about the myriad of different advisors out there who are all eager to help you. There are many good advisors and a bunch of mediocre ones too. From the information you learn in this book, you should be in a position to decide if an advisor will add value to your investment program or not. Pay attention to how the advisor gets paid to see if there are any possible conflicts of interest lurking in the background. Assess your comfort level with the individual and, if possible, get personal recommendations from existing clients. And if you buy mutual funds, buy no-load funds. (There, I said it again!)

Keeping Your Money Safe

'm sure you've heard the stories, or seen them on television, where some unscrupulous salesman gets a hold of the unsuspecting retiree on the phone and manages to convince him or her to buy some penny stock that is about to go through the roof. Another tempting distraction is the general category of stock tips. Everyone has one. Someone you know will claim to know of a major event that is about to happen at a company whose stock you should buy now. I almost feel the need to apologize to you for bringing up these schemes since I'm sure you know better, but I also feel that it would be unconscionable not to.

Let me summarize these points and move on: Never, ever listen to a sales pitch for an investment on the phone or in an email. I know that some of those scheming sales pitches have become very sophisticated and convincing. These folks know that the potential victim is going to be suspicious and they tailor the message to that fact. But don't listen. They don't know you, don't care about you, and just want you to buy some investments so they can earn a commission assuming, that is, that they are not out to just steal your money.

As for the stock tips: Do not act on stock tips no matter how good you consider the source. Your chances of winning at this game are very poor. For every one of these that might work out, 100 of them will be a wonderful opportunity for you to lose money in a hurry. So pass up the opportunity to make a quick buck from a stock tip. You will be happier for it. If you are tempted by stock tips, resist the temptation and go out and spend a few bucks on lottery tickets instead.

Now, let's talk about some other precautions we all need to take to keep our money safe. To begin, I am talking here about the safety of our assets from theft or failure of an investment firm, not safety from losses resulting from bad investment decisions. Managing investment risk is an important part of this book and I covered that subject extensively in the earlier chapters. In this section, I want to acquaint you with how your money should be entrusted to those who are advising you and what precautions you need to take to protect your assets.

Securities Investor Protection Corporation (SIPC)

When you deposit money in a commercial bank, you will likely see the legend "FDIC Insured." The Federal Deposit Insurance Corporation regulates commercial banks and also offers U.S. government insurance on bank deposits, generally up to an amount of $100,000. So if you own a bank certificate of deposit (CD) or open a checking account, you are generally covered against loss if your bank goes out of business or otherwise fails up to the amount of the FDIC insurance.

Securities firms have a similar type of insurance called Securities Investor Protection Corporation (SIPC). Like the FDIC, this government organization offers protection to investors with accounts at brokerage firms who are members and display the SIPC logo.

Note, however, that SIPC does not protect you from *investment* losses. The protection is against the theft of your securities or the bankruptcy of your securities firm where your assets are held. The insurance is generally limited to a total of $500,000 per customer of which no more than $100,000 can be in cash. Note too that while most types of securities are covered, typically stocks, bonds, and cash, more exotic securities—like commodity contracts and futures—are not covered. Most large brokerage firms offer at no additional cost supplemental insurance over and above the SIPC limits. Ask about this coverage if your securities account is over $500,000. Once you have checked into this coverage and you understand it, the safety of your deposits of securities and cash at a brokerage firm should not be an area of concern.

> **SIPC does not protect you from investment losses. The protection is against the theft of your securities or the bankruptcy of your securities firm where your assets are held.**

What's a Custodian?

Let's say you picked a portfolio from Chapter 7 consisting of some mutual funds and ETFs. To buy the ETFs you will likely need to open a securities account with a brokerage firm like Merrill Lynch or Smith Barney. Once the account is opened, you will write a check to the brokerage firm to be deposited into your account. At that point, the brokerage firm becomes the custodian of your assets. In other words, they are the keeper of your wealth in the form of cash or securities.

The way to understand how the custodial relationship works is to mentally separate in your mind the notion of what you are investing in and where your investments are being held. The money you send to buy shares from the mutual fund company doesn't actually go to the mutual fund; it goes to an account you open with the custodial institution. (State Street Corporation

There is rarely a need for your financial advisor to handle your money. The advisor *advises*. Period.

in Boston, founded in 1792, is the largest mutual fund custodian in the world with over $12 trillion of assets in custody.) Commercial banks also offer custody services, but unlike most brokerage firms, they charge extra for it. In general, you may be better off keeping your assets with a reputable brokerage firm.

I know this may sound obvious, but in the context of dealing with a financial advisor, keep in mind that there is rarely a need for your financial advisor to handle your money. The advisor *advises*. Period. Your financial advisor or consultant can help you with the *transfer* of your assets, but they must remain in the custody of a reputable, solid firm that offers custody services. Investment risk is something you should worry about. You should not have to worry about the safety of the assets you buy. If you ensure that your assets are in custody at a reliable firm, you can stop worrying about it.

Holding Stocks

If you buy shares of stock, there are two ways you can hold them: in the brokerage firm's name in an account you have at a brokerage investment firm, or in your own name.

If you get a monthly statement from your brokerage firm that lists all of your stocks in the holdings section of the statement, you have authorized your broker to hold the stocks for you. When you do this, the stocks are not registered in your name. The company you are invested in doesn't really know who you are. These securities are said to be in "street name," that is, in the name of the brokerage firm where you have opened an account and the securities you own are in it. (*Street name* is an old term referring to Wall Street, where most of the brokerage firms used to be located.)

The advantage of holding securities in this manner is that when you decide to sell a particular stock, you enter the order online, or you call your broker, tell him to sell the stock and that's all there is to it. The stock is already in your account, in street name, so nothing else needs to be done except to enter the order.

If you elect to hold the stock yourself, at the time you enter the order to buy the stock you would instruct your broker to have the stock registered in your own name. When you go this route, the broker will arrange for the company to record your name as an owner of the company which in turn will issue a stock certificate to you in your name. That stock certificate will be sent to you, printed in lots of green ink with elaborate designs and pictures of eagles and whatnot. You will henceforth receive communications directly from the company and if the company issues dividends, the company will send the checks directly to you. If the stock is in street name, the dividends will go to your broker, who will credit the dividend amount to your securities account. Similarly, if there are developments at the company whose stock you now own in your own name, the company will communicate the information directly to you. Of course, you will want to take care that the stock certificate is in a safe place under lock and key. Should you decide to sell it, you will not only have to place the order, you will have to dig out the stock certificate and take it to the broker to be processed in connection with the sale.

As you can see from the above example, owning stocks in your own name can be a major pain in the neck. Yet some individuals insist on keeping their certificates because they are concerned that if something happened to their brokerage firm, they would lose the stock. As I mentioned earlier, this is a very unlikely scenario given the protection afforded by both the SIPC

If you buy shares of stock, there are two ways you can hold them: in the brokerage firm's name in an account you have at a brokerage investment firm, or in your own name.

insurance and the additional insurance provided by most brokerage firms. But some people will not find sufficient comfort in this explanation and they will insist on keeping their stock certificates where they can look at them periodically.

Summing Up

With a few sensible precautions, the safety of your assets should not occupy a great deal of your time and attention. Indeed, your attention should be focused on ensuring that you have made the best possible investment decisions in your effort to build the winning portfolio that will make you rich.

Here are the points to remember about keeping your assets safe:

- Don't listen to stock tips or sales pitches from salesmen on the phone or the Internet.
- Know and understand the role of the custodian of your securities and cash.
- Make sure that your custodian is insured to a level that protects all of your assets.

Summing It All Up

In this concluding chapter, I want to do something more than just sum up the information I have shared with you about building your winning portfolio. My intention is to have this chapter serve as a quick refresher course. As such, this chapter will highlight the most important points you need to have handy as you embark on your investment future. So keep the book around, and come back here any time you need a quick refresher.

Let's start with something to get you motivated: Will I get rich? The answer is: YES! YES! YES! Just stick to the plan. The evidence and historical data make a very convincing case that persistence and regular additions to your portfolio will ensure your success. History is very much on your side.

Why doesn't everybody get rich if it's really that simple, you might ask? The answer: For a variety of reasons, most people never learn how to invest properly, or they learn and forget, or they lack the persistence and discipline to stick with it. In some ways, this isn't surprising. It takes both emotional and intellectual fortitude to stay in the stock market at times when all the pundits are warning you that stocks are overpriced, the market is too risky, and stocks start tumbling. And most people who sell out never get back in, or get back in at the wrong time. To believe in market timing—that is, getting in and out of the stock market—you have to believe that there are people who can accurately predict the future. And if you get out of the market, you have to be right not once, but twice, to be successful. You have to get out at the right time, and then you have to get back in at the right time. A number of investors try to do that. The vast majority fail. And that's another good reason why so few people get rich buying and selling stocks.

You will build your portfolio using the principles you learned earlier in the book. There is a wealth of academic knowledge in the field of finance to help us do this correctly. We have a history of over 80 years of solid data on stock market performance. Here is a summary of the basic rules you need to follow in assembling your winning portfolio.

Asset Allocation

As a result of a prominent and widely misunderstood study of asset allocation started in the 1980s, we conclude that of all the decisions you may make about your portfolio—including what stocks or funds to pick, when to get in or out of the market, or finding some brilliant stock market guru to advise you along the way—the single most important decision you, or anyone else, makes is the asset allocation. That decision involves how much of your money goes into the different types of investments, like domestic or international stocks, bonds, commodities, and anything else you might choose to invest in. The various portfolios from which you will choose in Chapter 7 take into account the importance of the asset allocation decision in determining your future returns.

Understand Risk

The way to manage stock market risk is to understand it. With knowledge comes confidence, and you need confidence to stay the course in growing your winning portfolio. You know that stocks will fluctuate. You also know that stocks have been the best performing asset in American history over long periods of time.

Diversify!

The key element in managing risk is diversification. By diversifying our portfolio, we spread the risk around. We learned that when you buy stocks, you are inevitably saddled with stock market risk. But we also learned that there are other types of risks in the stock market that we can do something about. We learned that large company stocks behave differently from small company stocks. We know that value stocks behave differently from growth stocks. So we can diversify these risks away by neutralizing them, that is, by owning both large and small company stocks, and growth and value stocks.

Be Patient!

The second element to managing risk is patience. Some history helps here. Remember our discussion in Chapter 2 on Standard and Poor's performance since 1928? Start any year you would like and ask yourself the following questions:

- What are the chances that I will make money in stocks over that five-year period? The answer: 74 percent.

- What are the chances of making money in the stock market in any 10-year period since 1928? Answer: 87 percent.
- What are the chances of making money in the stock market in any 20-year period since 1928? Answer: 95 percent.

And remember that this period of time since 1928 covers the Great Depression! These statistics should give you the confidence you need to stick to your investment program and get rich.

Should You Buy Stocks or Mutual Funds?

You have a big choice to make in assembling your winning portfolio: Will it be populated with stocks you either pick yourself or through a brokerage firm, or will you choose some mutual funds and let the fund managers pick the stocks for you (for a small fee)? And you may recall, I highly recommend that you use mutual funds for the equity portion of your portfolio rather than choose stocks yourself. And this is why: If you choose to buy stocks yourself, explain to me (and more important, to yourself) how you are going to do better than the professional money managers who do this 8 or 10 hours a day? I'm afraid I don't know how either!

Load Funds versus No-Load Funds

There are good load funds and good no-load funds. So why buy a load fund that costs you much more to own? So remember, avoid load funds!

Active versus Passive Investing

Active investing refers to investing with an objective to beat the stock market's performance. Passive investing describes the process of investing in order to get the same return as the stock market.

Some areas of the stock market are harder to beat than others. Don't fight it. The large company indexes, like the S&P 500 and the Dow Jones Average, are very tough to beat since it is hard to gain an information edge on developments at those widely followed, large companies. So I recommend that when investing in large-cap stocks, you not try to beat the market but buy an index fund instead. The fund expenses will be a lot cheaper and you won't take the chance that some active fund manager will underperform the stock market in his unsuccessful attempt to try to beat it. For other types of stocks, pick active managers using the fund screening process you learned in Chapter 5, or another screening program like it.

Building the Winning Portfolio

Your personal winning portfolio allocation will be a function of two primary factors:

1. Your time frame
2. Your risk tolerance

The longer the time frame, the better your chances of achieving true wealth are. Your risk tolerance is a matter of personal choice and a strong element of psychology. Online risk-tolerance tests (like the ones we discussed in Chapter 6) are useful tools to help you determine how much risk you are comfortable with.

Once you have decided on the two factors, risk tolerance and time frame, you are prepared to choose one of the portfolio allocations in Chapter 7. Your allocation is likely to include different types of domestic and international stocks, bonds, and some allocation to energy and gold if your portfolio is large enough.

Here are some summary points to remember when building your winning portfolio:

- Asset allocation is the single most important decision we will make in building the portfolio. If the three most important rules in real estate are location, location, location, then the three most important rules in building a winning portfolio are diversification, diversification, diversification.
- It is very difficult to beat the market's performance, but that doesn't mean we shouldn't try if we do so selectively and intelligently.
- For the largest part of the portfolio, mutual funds will be the best choice to achieve growth and diversification.
- Buy no-load funds. Your role in life is NOT to provide a good living to mutual fund salesmen.

Maintenance and Upkeep

Like most things in life, your portfolio will require upkeep and maintenance. The two most important elements are:

1. Benchmarking
2. Rebalancing

Benchmarking

It is very, very important that you know how the people you are paying to manage your money are doing— whether they are mutual fund managers, portfolio managers, or financial advisors who help you with your investments. To find out, you must have benchmarks you can use to evaluate your managers' and the portfolio's performance. Your managers should be benchmarked against an appropriate index. Over long periods of time, your fund should beat the index or it isn't worth the effort and the money to pay the manager's fee.

Rebalancing

Your portfolio from Chapter 7 is carefully designed to reach specific investment goals. Over time, the percentage allocation to each asset class is certain to change, if only because the asset classes will grow at different rates. About once a year, consider rebalancing your portfolio to their original allocations. Do this by selling a portion of those funds that have risen to a higher percentage of your portfolio than the original percentage allocation and adding funds to those that have fallen below their original allocations to bring those allocations back up to where they should be.

Parting Thoughts

This is the toughest part to write since it is a bit like saying goodbye to an old friend. After all, we have spent a fair amount of time together and I hope I've done my part in helping you get started on your winning portfolio. I have brought four decades of experience in the industry to bear in sharing these lessons with you. My career as an investment professional covers years when many unthinkable catastrophes occurred, including the

Kennedy assassination, the 1973–1974 major market decline, and the 1987 stock market crash. More recently, we suffered through the horrendous events of September 11, 2001, and three straight declining years in the stock market in 2000, 2001, and 2002, totaling a cumulative decline of over 40 percent.

And you know what? We survived it all. The takeaway from this is simply that through thick and thin, your investments in stocks and bonds, gold, and energy will very likely continue to grow and make you rich.

So be patient. Think rich. Stick to it. You will get there, and I'll be proud of you!

I constantly wonder who reads these inevitable acknowledgment pages. Of course, I expect those acknowledged in a book to read the acknowledgments, but what about the rest of you?

I think most of you know that the author of any book doesn't work in a vacuum. Let me start with my collaborators. These are some of the people I work with at Lynx Investment Advisory who are experts in their respective fields and who generously lent their expertise to this book, mostly in their spare time. Allow me to introduce you to them:

Matthew D. Gelfand, Ph.D, CFA, CFP®

Matt serves as the Chief Investment Officer for Consulting at Lynx Investment Advisory, LLC. He has participated in the investment management industry for more than 18 years and has been a practicing economist for more than eight years. Matt received his BA from Yale University (*magna cum laude*) and PhD from the University of Pennsylvania, both in economics. He has earned the CFA designation, and is a CFP professional.

Umer Farouq, CFA

Umer is Vice President – Research at Lynx Investment Advisory, LLC. He has more than 15 years of experience in the financial services industry in a variety of capacities, including due diligence, performance reporting, quantitative analysis, and application development. Umer holds a CFA charter and an MBA from St. Louis University, and a BS/BA from Washington University with a minor in Economics. If you like the charts in the book, thank Umer.

Vipin Sahijwani, CFA

Vipin is Vice President – Research at Lynx Investment Advisory, LLC. He has more than 10 years of experience in portfolio management, investment modeling, market analysis and econometrics. Vipin holds a CFA charter and has a MBA from the George Washington University, Washington, D.C., and a master's degree in Market Research and Forecasting from the Center for Management Development in India. He also has a BA in Economics from the University of Delhi, India.

Deborah L. Pierdominici

Deborah is responsible for assisting the Research Department and maintaining the research database at Lynx Investment Advisory, LLC. Deborah is a graduate of American University with a BA in Law and Society and an MA in Philosophy and Social Policy.

I am grateful to my friend Yvette Romero at Kaplan Publishing who suggested to me that I write this book; to Shannon Berning at Kaplan, who guided me through the acquisition process; to Dominique Polfliet, a highly skilled production editor; and to my talented editor, Monica Lugo, who is wise beyond her years and who I hope will remember me when she becomes famous in the industry.

Family and close friends are also a source of inspiration, counsel and moral support during the sometimes long process of writing a book. My "trophy wife" of

Acknowledgments

45 years, Ann Tanous was as gracious and helpful as she always is, to me, to our colleagues at work, and to our family. These include three children, Christopher, Helene and Will, all in different fields of endeavor not involving finance. Daughter Helene Bartilucci is a mother of three adorable little girls, and son-in-law Paul Bartilucci had the good sense to recognize that finance is, after all, a worthwhile and fulfilling occupation. He is a Director at Citi Global Wealth Management.

My dearest friends, Al and Tina Coury, endured yet another cruise with Ann and me (our 18th together), this time to Alaska off-season, while I got away from the office to finish a couple of the more difficult chapters in the book.

Thanks to Greg Headley and Michael McCaffrey at DFA, who helped with the important charts I used to show the performance of mutual funds versus the S&P 500. And thanks once again Robert Dintzner of DFA who also helped me with my first investment book, *Investment Gurus.*

My agent and friend of over thirty years, Theron Raines, has provided wisdom and guidance of incalculable value.

Thanks to you the reader for believing enough in this project to acquire the book, read it, and hopefully follow the advice found herein.

And a big hug and kisses to the three young ladies to whom this book is dedicated, Olivia Bartilucci, and twins Lilly and Isabella Bartilucci who are—as I know you already guessed—my three beautiful granddaughters!

Index